How to Train Hunting Dogs to Hunt Rabbits and Coon

How to Train Hunting Dogs to Hunt Rabbits and Coon

Walter James

Copyright © 2010 by Walter James.

Library of Congress Control Number: 2010909172
ISBN: Hardcover   978-1-4535-2623-1
                 Softcover   978-1-4535-2622-4
                 Ebook   978-1-4535-2624-8

All rights reserved. No part of this book may be reproduced or transmitted in any form or by any means, electronic or mechanical, including photocopying, recording, or by any information storage and retrieval system, without permission in writing from the copyright owner.

This book was printed in the United States of America.

To order additional copies of this book, contact:
Xlibris Corporation
1-888-795-4274
www.Xlibris.com
Orders@Xlibris.com
81603

Contents

Amazing Joe 7

Chapter 2 29

Chapter 3 33

Joe's Hunting Mate (Dot) 51

How to Train a Rabbit Dog 53

How to Train Coon Dogs At Six Months Old to Track Coons 58

A Coonhound Dog Blue's And Ring's Last Hunt 64

An Angry Raccoon 79

Amazing Joe

In the year 1956, Ted was tired of hunting with men and their so-called rabbit dogs. He said to Jack, "I want me a young dog. I will train it."

Jack laughed and said, "Ted, you don't know how to train a dog."

Ted replied, "When I get one, you will see for yourself what I can do."

Jack replied, "I will take you where you can get a dog if you just want a dog."

That Saturday morning, they went to Oakland County Humane Society. There he found himself a good-looking dog. He was a bluetick mixed with beagle. Ted bought him for ten dollars, and they brought him home with them. He fed him good for two days. After that, Ted turned him loose. He named him Joe, and when he called him, he would come.

The thing he liked to do most was to slide his food pan around in the yard. His front left paw would sit in the empty pan, tilted against his leg, and with the help of his head, he would hold it and run across the backyard growling as though the empty pan was his enemy.

Several days later, Jack said, "Let's take him out with my dog tomorrow. He might be already trained."

Jack and Ted took their dogs out that Tuesday evening. Jack's dog ran a rabbit for two hours. Ted's dog didn't know how to hunt. But he outran Jack's dog, got in front of him, and tried to look into his mouth while he was barking.

Jack yelled, "Look at Joe! He thinks the rabbit is in my dog's mouth." He started laughing. Then he said, "Man, you have yourself some kind of hunting dog. Whenever we go hunting this fall, please don't take this big thing in the woods with us. I don't want him fighting with my dog. If he hurts my dog, I will have to shoot him. I am going to tell you something about Old Joe. He will make a good show dog. Get him in a show, and no dog could beat him rolling a pan. He can roll a pan better than I can. Now you take my dog, Ben, he knows how to hunt."

Angrily Ted said, "Joe is going to hunt! I don't care what you say."

Jack laughed so hard; he had to sit down to keep from falling. He stopped laughing long enough to say, "What did you say?" Then he laughed again.

Ted caught Joe, put his leash on him, and they started for home. Jack called his dog, then he said, "Ted, look at Ben! This is a hunting dog. Watch how he follows me without a leash." Ted knew then that he had a lot of work to do training Joe.

Jack told the other fellows about Ted's dog. Some of them came by just to see Joe roll his pan around in the yard. Man, could that dog roll that pan!

Joe loved to eat, so Ted knew what he had to do. He drove up and down some of the main highways early in the morning until he found a rabbit that had been killed by a car. He picked him up, brought him home, cut his head off, and pulled the fur off his neck. He held the rabbit against the fence where Joe could smell it. The more Joe smelled it, the closer he tried to get to it.

Ted took the neck part and pushed it through the fence. Joe began to chew on it. Ted let him get a good taste of it, and then took it away from him. He started hollering. Ted knew then that he was going to be a good hunting dog.

He tied a string around the rabbit, dragged him around the house, into the front yard. Then he hid him under a hedge bush.

He opened the gate and let Joe out. Joe followed that drag until he found the rabbit. Ted took it from him and put him back in the pen; then he made a long drag. He went out of the yard, across the street, on down the hill to the woods, bringing it back in a different direction. Then he hung him in a pine tree. He came back, turned Joe loose, and Joe followed that drag every step of the way until he found that rabbit. He wanted to eat him real bad. Now, Ted knew that he would hunt. He gave him the rabbit to eat.

He then began taking him out behind the golf course every day. Joe got better and better. By the time hunting season came, he was good. Jack would often ask Ted, "How is that show dog doing?"

Ted would say to him, "He's only good at rolling his food pan."

Jack teased, "When you enter him in the show, he should win first prize with his looks alone!" Then he would laugh. Just before leaving, he said, "That big, old pretty dog could not eat bread off my table. It's clear that he's not gonna be able to hunt October 20 when hunting season open."

Now the hunting season had begun. The fellows had bought their license, and they were ready to go hunting. At 7:00 a.m., Jack and Ted rode together since they lived right next door to each other. Jack brought his dog over and put him in Ted's car trunk, and Ted put Joe in too. Jack joked, "We are going to clean up those woods today. We have the show dog with us!"

Ted growled in reply, "Don't worry, he will hunt."

Jack replied, "You know that I know all about his hunting!"

They arrived at the state park's hunting grounds at 8:00 a.m. They parked their cars in the parking lot that the state provided for hunters to use. They got out of their cars and let the dogs out too. The dogs got plenty of fresh air while they put on their jackets and loaded their guns. Everyone was ready to go hunting!

The day was cool and crisp. The autumn sun caught the top of the trees, and the fresh cried out to be inhabited by hunters.

Joe and Ted were on the edge of a great day. They were partners, and now the hunt had begun. Some of the men were at the edge of the field walking in the tall grass, and the others were walking through the woods. They were all walking slowly, watching and listening for the sound of a rabbit running through the grass and leaves. It's hard for the hunters to see the small rabbit when he is in his bed.

Tension filled the cool morning air; all were looking hard. Every man wanted to kill the most rabbits, except Ted; all he wanted was for Joe to become a good tracking dog.

The grass was wet from the dew; this was good for the dogs. They could smell the rabbit's scent better. There were no clouds in the sky. The sun was shining, and the wind was still. This was a good day for hunting.

As they were walking, a rabbit jumped out of his bed and ran through the tall grass. No one had a chance to shoot at him.

They called the dogs over and put them on his track. The dogs could not pick up his scent. It was too soon. The fumes from the cars bothered their smelling abilities. After being in the fresh air for about twenty minutes, they would be all right.

Ted went over to the rabbit bed carrying Joe with him. Jack started laughing and said, "What are you carrying the show dog over there for? We didn't come out here to see a show, we came to kill rabbits."

Ted pushed Joe's head into the place where the rabbit had been sitting. Joe started digging. Ted took him by the collar, turned him around, patted him on the back, and said, "Catch him, boy!" Joe went trotting through the grass with his head on the ground and soon starting barking. His barking sounded like hollering. This dog seemed determined to embarrass Ted; even his bark wasn't right.

Jack yelled, "Who's hurting Pretty Boy?" The other fellows started laughing. Joe was going farther and farther away.

Finally Jack said, "We're not going to catch any rabbits today with that dog hollering."

Bob said sharply, "No dog is hunting, but Pretty Boy!"

Jack shouted, "That's no rabbit! Don't pay Pretty Boy any attention."

As they walked through the woods, Joe was still running the rabbit. He went around the lake and came back. Dan said, "The rabbit is coming your way, Jack!"

Jack asked, "What rabbit?" Dan told him, "The one Hollering Boy is running." "Man, what are you talking about?" Jack inquired.

Dan said, "He's heading straight for you!" Everyone stood still; the breaking of dead sticks and shaking of bushes would cause the rabbit to turn and go in another direction. The rabbit came close to Jack, and Jack killed him.

Jack exclaimed, "What's wrong with the other dogs? They did not run this rabbit! If old Hollering Boy keeps this up, he's going to make your dog look bad, Dan."

Dan said, "What about your dog?"

As they walked, soon another rabbit jumped up in front of Chuck and ran about fifty feet. Chuck aimed his gun at the rabbit and pulled the trigger. The rabbit jumped up in the air and fell on his side and started kicking.

Jack hollered with a loud voice, "Did you kill him?" "I got him," Chuck answered.

Jack said, "Everybody listen, the next rabbit that gets up, do not shoot him, I want the dogs to run him. If they can't track him, it has to be something wrong with them."

As they walked slowly through the fields and woods, another rabbit jumped up. That little fellow was really running; all you could see was that white tail of his going through the bushes.

The rabbit got up in front of Dan. Dan called two of the dogs over and put them on his trail. Those dogs started barking like they were looking at him. You could hear the other dogs running toward those dogs. Soon all the dogs started barking.

Ben with his deep voice, "Whoo, whoo, whoooo!" was leading the pack. Jack yelled with a loud voice, "Catch him, Ben." Then he said, "Boys, that is a rabbit dog you hear now. Just listen to that voice. Now he feels better, we're going to get some rabbits today!"

Chuck said, "Men, you haven't heard anything, just wait until Spot takes over."

Jack growled, "No way is he going to outtrack Ben." Ben was doing his best to stay ahead of Spot. Spot was right behind him, with high-pitched little yelps. Chuck yelled, "Take the lead, Spot!" You could hear Ben and Spot about two hundred feet ahead of the other dogs. Poor Joe was behind. He was howling all the way. *Ooh, oooh, ooooh.*

Jack hollered, "Ted, what is Joe doing? He's gotten lost from the other dogs. You better go and get him." Ted replied, "Don't worry. He's tracking too!" Jack screamed, "The only thing Pretty Boy is tracking is Ben." Then he laughed, "Haw haw!" Ted yelled, "You just keep laughing. Before the hunting season is over, you'll change that tune of yours."

While they were standing there talking, waiting for the dogs to bring the rabbit back, Ben overran the track, and Spot took the lead. Jack stopped laughing. Spot was coming straight back to us.

Chuck screamed with a loud voice, "Jack, listen to that music. That's Spot coming this way, and Ben is following him." Then he started jumping up and down laughing. He yelled, "Catch him, Spot. Catch him, boy. I will buy you a steak for dinner."

Spot was trying hard to catch the rabbit. His feet were turning over the leaves as he ran through the woods. His head parted the grass when he went through the field. It sounded like he was barking every time he picked up his feet. He was running like he was running for his life. That rabbit was moving so fast he looked like a brown ball rolling through the woods. Chuck's heart was bubbling over with joy. Spot had taken the lead. Jack was disappointed. Ben was trailing Spot. Jack was screaming, "Take the lead, Ben. Pass him, Ben. Come on, Ben, you can do it."

Bell yelled, "Shut up, blabbermouth. Your dog is getting old. He has lost some of that speed he used to have."

Ted did not say a word. He was listening to Joe bring up the rear, saying to himself, "Someday he will be the number one dog. He is tracking that rabbit every step of the way."

Fred hollered with a loud voice, "He's coming your way, Chuck." Chuck stood still, not moving a muscle. Soon he raised his gun and went bang, bang, and bang. He said, "I got him. Spot ran him straight to me. Now that's what I call a rabbit dog."

Jack replied, "You shot up half the woods trying to kill him. The way you were shooting, I thought I was back on the front line. I started looking for the enemy!"

Chuck said, "I got what I was shooting at. You can call it anything you want to. For me, it's meat on my table."

Jack asked, "Does anyone see Ben? I want to be sure that Chuck didn't shoot him." Chuck answered, "He's over here trying to get my rabbit. You should feed him. He's hungry."

As we stood still shooting the bullshit, Joe came up on the rabbit's track, howling all the way. He didn't stop until he got to the spot where Chuck killed the rabbit; then he went around in a circle trying to find the rabbit.

Chuck hollered, "Pretty Boy has made it here."

Jack yelled, "What is he doing? Is he trying to find Ben?"

Chuck answered, "Naw, man. He's trying to find the rabbit. He's not paying the dog any attention. He's going around in circles trying to find the rabbit."

Ted spoke in a loud voice asking Chuck to let Joe smell the rabbit. Chuck took the rabbit out of his bag, called Joe to him, and let him smell it. Joe grabbed it. He had to make him let go of the rabbit. Chuck hollered, "Pretty Boy's not hunting for fun. He wants to eat this rabbit."

Ted called Joe over and patted him on the head and said, "Good boy. Now let's find another rabbit." They started walking. Then Ted said, "Let's find some rabbits, men." As everyone started walking, Tom Jones said, "C'mon, guys, let's do some hunting. Chuck and Jack are acting like they are at the racetrack. We have been waiting all the summer for this day. To me I don't care whose dog can track the fastest or who's the best hunter. I came out here to kill rabbits."

Chuck replied, "I am happy to know that Spot showed Ben up. I don't care if he doesn't ever run another rabbit." Jack replied, "It's time for him to do something. Ben's growing old. He has trained every dog that's out here. Since Ben has showed me that he can track, I am going to show you guys how to shoot."

The dew had dried on the grass and leaves. As they walked through the forest, you could hear their feet crunching them. Whenever they would get close to a rabbit, the rabbit would start moving himself in his bed. The noise made him nervous; soon he would jump out of his bed and run for a thicker place to hide. Sometimes the hunters would see them; some would slip out between the men going back the way they came. Those that moved out of their bed and moved in front of the hunters, their trails were often picked up by the dogs. The dogs always went in front of the hunters. Now, the hunters are moving slowly down one side of the swamp to their right, listening for a rabbit running and looking hard to see one sitting or running. The hunters were happy, knowing that all dogs were able to smell a track. Soon a rabbit ran in front of Jack; that little fellow was really running.

Jack raised his gun to his shoulder, pushed his safety off, pointing his gun at the rabbit, putting his head against the stock of his gun, closing his left eye looking down the barrel with his other eye, taking aim quickly, then he squeezed the trigger. The gun went *boom!* The rabbit flipped over on his side and started kicking. Someone hollered, "Did you get him?" Jack said, "All I have to do is point my gun at him, and he'll fall out. They know a hunter when they see one. You guys have been hunting with me long enough to know that I do not miss." Bill said, "There's that ole loudmouth again. He cannot keep his mouth closed." Jack replied, "You all know that I am the best shooter that you've ever gone hunting with, so why don't you admit it."

Fred said, "Put your gun where your mouth is, and let's see how many rabbits we can kill today." While they were talking, Ben opened up. The dog was barking like he was looking at a rabbit. Everyone was looking and listening for the rabbit. Soon all the dogs were barking, even Old Joe. With all the noise the dogs were making, the rabbit had no other choice but to move. Soon there were two shots. *Boom! Boom!*

A scream was heard. Ben said, "He's coming your way, Bill." A few seconds later, Bill's gun went *boom! boom!* He yelled, "Ted, Ted, he's coming your way." Ted stood there watching. Soon he could see the rabbit running on the dry leaves. The dogs were two hundred feet behind him. Ted raised his gun, took the safety off, and aimed it at the rabbit, letting him run closer. Soon he squeezed the trigger, and the gun went off. The rabbit fell over on his left side and began to kick. He walked over to him, called the dogs over, letting them smell it. "That's a good boy." He put the rabbit in his game bag, saying, "Let's walk on farther." As they went a little farther, another rabbit got up in front of Ted. As the rabbit ran, Ted raised his gun to his right shoulder, pointing at him as fast as he could, squeezed the trigger and killed the rabbit.

Jack screamed for the dogs. "You know you missed him." Ted said, "I killed him. Let the dogs keep on hunting." Jack replied,

"I don't believe it, hold him up where I can see it?" Ted held him up. Jack looked at him. He said, "Boys, he got another one. We've got to watch him. He's trying to kill all the game." Ted said, "Men, whenever a rabbit comes by you, and you don't kill him, if he comes my way, I will."

Chuck said, "Look who's talking. He had two lucky shots, now he's running off at the mouth." Bill screamed, "I would have killed that rabbit, but the sun blinded me. I just shot the way he went." Ted replied, "One excuse is better than none. Now let's hunt and quit talking. I am going to kill more game than anyone."

As they were walking through the woods, Ted saw a rabbit sitting in his bed. He passed by him as if he didn't see him. After he had walked about twenty feet, he turned slowly, raising his gun again to his right shoulder, aiming it at his head. Jack saw him and yelled, "Ted, what are you going to do?" Ted squeezed the trigger; then he said, "I hit what I shoot. I do not walk by many rabbits sitting in their beds." Then he screamed with a loud voice, "Now, men, you can hunt like Jack wants you to, or hunt the best way you can, if you can shoot a rabbit in his bed, that's one that the dogs cannot track."

Now, the hunt was getting good. The dogs have jumped on a rabbit and were running. Every dog was barking; that was music to the hunter's ears, just hearing the sound of dogs barking. Even Joe was with them, howling. He's hunting his heart out.

This was something to hear; the hunters were waiting, watching, and listening for the rabbits to come back. They could hear the dogs hammering down. "Hammering down" is a word that hunters use when their dogs were barking while they were tracking. The dogs were going around in a circle. Bill said, "The rabbit is over there in that muck patch running round and round in it. Let's go and kill him." As they started walking toward the dogs, Jack was walking through some tall grass, and two large cock pheasants flew up right beside him. This scared him so bad, until he could not move for about thirty seconds. By the time he came to himself, the birds were out of shooting distance.

Bill hollered, "Why didn't you shoot those birds?" Chuck yelled, "How could he shoot, he was too busy using the seat of his pants for the bathroom."

Jack laughed, "Haw haw!" Then he said, "Those birds did scare me. All I was thinking about was that Ben is running. Tell Chuck there is nothing wrong with my pants." They hurried over to where the dogs were. They placed themselves around that muck patch where the dogs were hunting. There was more than one rabbit moving around in there. The men can only get a glimpse of the rabbit as he passed by under the bushes; the men would shoot the way they saw him go, hoping they would get lucky and kill one. The little bushes were one feet to four feet tall.

The men tried hard to kill the rabbits; they began to get discouraged. Ted could see all the men but Jack.

Ted yelled, "Jack, where are you?"

Jack hollered, "Back over here, be quiet, I am killing rabbits."

He was lying down on the ground under the tall brushes. He was able to see the rabbits better and kill them. Ted replied, "Jack, get up off that ground. We're not in the army. Stand up where you can be seen, and no one will shoot you, accidentally." Jack yelled, "I cannot help it because you men don't know how to hunt. On second thought, I'd better get up, before one of you guys get jealous and shoot me. Then I would have to kill somebody."

He got up laughing and said, "I killed four rabbits since we've been over here. How many have you killed?" Ted said, "I haven't had a decent shoot. Every time I see one, he runs back in the thicket before I can shoot." Ted yelled, "Men, get your dogs. We'll go somewhere else, where it's not so thick. Those dogs can run a rabbit all day long in this place, and we will never get a decent shot or kill him." Fred replied, "I was hoping that someone would suggest that we leave from here."

They took their dogs and went across the woods to the other side. The hunting was good. That day Jack killed the most rabbits. Everyone killed rabbits. On their way home, Jack told the boys that he was going to teach Ted how to train Joe to track like Ben.

Then he spoke these words, "Pretty Boy fooled me, and today was the first time he ever hunted. He didn't hunt like a dog just learning to hunt. He hunted just as long as those trained dogs. Old loudmouth is happy. He killed the most game. He can't stop talking because he thinks he knows everything."

He said that they would take Joe out Wednesday evening. Ben would teach him how to track fast. The next time they take him out, old Spot will have to track faster than he does. Jack was doing a lot of talking; he didn't know that Ted was not going to wait on him to help train Joe. Ted knew how to train a dog to hunt; whatever he wanted him to hunt, if it's rabbits, birds, raccoons, or foxes. He learned this when he was growing up. Every time Ted looked at Joe, he saw something better than a pretty large show dog. No one had taken time to teach him how to hunt; he learned himself how to roll his food pan around in the yard. Now he has someone who will teach him to hunt. Within Ted's heart and mind, he saw Joe tracking better than any dog that he had hunted with in the state of Michigan.

Ted's mind went back to the last dog that he owned in the state of Alabama in the year of 1942. His name was Rover; he was some rabbit dog. "I will train Joe myself and put Jack's mouth to shame," thought Ted.

One night in the month of September, the year of 1942, Uncle Johnnie came from Auburn, Alabama, to Tuskegee, Alabama, to see Ted. He brought him a redbone hound dog.

He told Ted, "I am giving you this dog. He is the best rabbit dog that I have, but if I keep him, he's going to get my coonhound killed. He dug a hole under the fence, and my two coon dogs followed him over on a poultry farm. They were running rabbits. The other dogs were shot with a .22 rifle. It did not kill him, however, it cost me a doctor bill."

Ted thought he had a good rabbit dog. He had been working with Mr. Brown who trained dogs. He had trained his dog to track whatever he wanted him to track. He took old Rover and tied him to the extra doghouse.

Johnnie said, "Don't worry about his rusty back. Someone poured something on his back, and his hair came off. Do not let that worry you. He is good." Ted looked at him; he was not a pretty dog. His back alone would make you change your mind about him. Ted took him.

Later on, he was glad that he did. That winter he had a chance to show his dog off. He was good too. The news spread about Ted's dog. There were lots of hunters who came to hunt with Ted. Rover would track a rabbit until someone killed him or he went into a hole. One day they were hunting when Ted's older brother went along. He took the gun. Ted went, but he had no gun. The dogs ran a rabbit for two hours; the men were shooting at him and missing.

Ted became angry; he said, "What are you all trying to do? Run my dog to death?" All the other dogs quit hunting and came out of the swamp. Twenty minutes later, here came a rabbit with Rover chasing close behind. The men were sitting on the side of the hill. Rover was so close that no one could shoot the rabbit without shooting the dog. He caught the rabbit. Sam had a large black hound. He was sitting on the side of the hill too. He heard the rabbit crying out. He ran over to Rover and jumped on him. Rover turned the rabbit loose and put a whooping on Sam's dog.

The rabbit got loose from Rover and ran back to Sam. Ted came out of the swamp as fast as he could to help his dog. He looked up on the side of the hill to his left. There he saw Rover all by himself running as fast as he could. He had quit barking. When he reached the top of the hill, there was a wagon road up there. He headed down the road. All the hunters were following him. He ran down the road for half a mile. He stopped and lay down. Ted got to him first with a stick in his hand. He looked down at his dog. There lay a live rabbit. He took his stick and killed it. Soon all the hunters were there. Talk about what a dog Rover was.

While they were deciding on what direction they were going, Buck's dog jumped on Rover. Rover got that dog down, and Ted had to take him off. Now Ted was really angry. He said, "My dogs and I are going home—before I have to kill some of these dogs."

The hunters asked him to stay. Ted said no. He took Rover and Mack and left. He thought that Mack was a good hunter, but old Rover showed them all up. Mack had been his number one dog. Mack was an all-around dog; he was used for herding hogs, cattle, and horses. He tried to do whatever Ted wanted him to do. He was a full-blooded pointer-bird dog.

He seldom hunted birds with him. Shells were rationed. This was during World War II, and everything was rationed. As the years passed, Ted became eighteen; he had to register for the army. He had a choice to go to the army or work for the government. Ted signed up to learn art welding at Tuskegee Institute for the government after he was trained. He was sent to the Mobile, Alabama, shipyard.

Jack thought that Ted was going to wait for Wednesday to come before he took Joe into the woods again. Monday morning, Ted got up early. He did not have to go to work until 11:00 p.m. He worked the midnight shift.

He took Joe out every morning—if it wasn't raining, Monday through Friday, behind the golf course. He knew that Joe had to learn how to track good. It was easy for a dog to track a young rabbit. Tracking an old rabbit is different. Ted stood at the edge of the swamp watching for the rabbit to come out on his side. Whenever a rabbit came out, he would call Joe and put him on his track. Joe hunted hard. He learned fast. Ted never turned down a chance to take his dog out with Jack. Jack told the boys that his dog was teaching Joe how to track. This did not worry Ted; he knew what he was doing. All the hunters were talking about Joe.

Ted was not satisfied yet; he wanted him to be the best dog in the woods. Now Joe lived in the house with Ted. Ted soon had him trained to go across the golf course and hunt by himself. When he came home in the morning, he would fix breakfast for Joe and himself; then he would send him hunting. Ted would awaken, and Joe was nowhere around. He would go across the golf course and get him.

This worked out good for one year. Joe stopped letting Ted catch him behind the golf course. Ted could hear him over there tracking his heart out. Ted got close enough to see and catch him. Joe would go in the thickest part of the swamp, stand still, and stop barking. When Ted would leave, he would start hunting again.

Now, Ted did not like this at all. He wanted Joe to hunt; he also wanted him to come when he called him. Joe stopped coming home. When Ted went to work, Joe would come home and sleep in the neighbor's doghouse and leave before Ted got home. He did this for two weeks before Ted had a day off, when he could catch him. Joe had gotten so good he was catching his own food. Ted caught him and put him in the dog pen.

As the years passed, Joe became the number one hunting dog. All the hunters hunted with him. They took their friends hunting with them. Sometimes when Ted was talking with some of the younger men at his job, those who like to hunt, he found out that a lot of them had been hunting with Joe.

Chuck did more hunting than the other hunters. He hunted more with Joe than anyone, and he would tell the young men that did not know Joe, that he was his dog, and that if they killed a rabbit and was not able to pick him up before Joe got there, that they do not try to pick him up. He also told them that Joe would not eat their rabbits and that he will not let any of the other dogs have it. He was going to bring him the rabbit and that he will give it to them.

Ted knew that he would do that when he took him hunting. When he first started doing this, some of the hunters wanted to shoot him. Joe did not care what size the swamp was nor how far Ted was from him. He would bring him the game. The fellows talked about Ted like he was a dog, saying he had trained Joe to steal their game.

Ted often told them he could not help it because Joe was the fastest dog in the woods and the largest. Then he would say that Joe was good, asking them, "Am I right?"

Bill said, "This guy is gone crazy. We got to get him admitted in the hospital." Then they all laughed, even Ted. Ted yelled, "That was a large rabbit you killed, Bill, and Joe brought him to me. I should have had a camera to take his picture. He looked good with that rabbit hanging half on one side and half on the other side of his mouth."

Bill replied, "The next time he does that, you are going to have a dead, dead dog." When he got behind Ted's back, he said to the other hunters, "I got to admit, Joe is good. He's always doing something different year, but he is crazy, don't ever try to put your hands on him, he will bite! He's like his master, he's crazy!"

When Ted would be listening to those young men talk, his mind would all the way be back to the time the same thing happened to him. What the men were saying about Chuck. Sometimes he would tell them that Joe was his dog, and other times he would act like he never knew him. Now the time had come for Joe to prove how good he could track on snow and ice.

Joe knew how to track on dry land and when it was wet. He knew how to look for rabbits in large bunches of grass, under small bushes, and the underbrush piles.

The question was going through Ted's mind, will he be able to track on snow and ice? They were hunting in snow six inches deep. The dogs were running good in the thick and underbrush. A rabbit came out and went across the hill. Ted saw him from a distance. He went to where he saw him and called Joe and put him on the track. Then he found out that Joe did not know how to track on snow. Joe was walking and looking at the rabbit's tracks in the snow, putting his nose in each track. He saw that day, that Joe would never be able to track in the snow. He'd never catch a rabbit like that; he caught Joe by the collar, pushing his head close to the snow. Joe followed. Soon he took off and passed Ted, tracking on his own. Now Ted could smile again.

Now the hunting was getting good. Joe was able to track on snow. They hunted until 5:00 p.m., then called it a day and went home.

As the hunting season passed on, Ted kept on hunting. Now the lakes were frozen. On the second Saturday in the month of February, Ted and his friends went hunting. The dogs were jumping rabbits. They would not run long before they would hold up.

Ted came to a small pond in the swamp; it was frozen, so he walked over it. He got halfway across. There were a lot of trees in the middle as he drew closer. A rabbit jumped off a stump in the middle of those trees. Ted called the dogs over and put them on the track. They acted like they couldn't smell the scent.

Bill said those dogs couldn't track on ice. Ted never said a word. He called Joe over, caught him by the collar, and put his nose on top of the stump; however, he was not able to track on ice. He went around the stump and around it. Ted looked at him and said, "Poor Joe." He reached out and caught a hold to his collar, pulling him along on the ice slipping and sliding, sometimes falling, but doing his best to keep Joe's nose on the ice. Soon Joe began to bark.

Ted turned him loose. Across the lake he went, doing his funny barking. Soon he had the rabbit on the run. The other hunters hollered as they looked at that big fellow go on that ice. Soon he ran the rabbit back. Ted killed him.

Bill said that's the first time he ever saw a dog track on ice. "What kind of dog tracks on ice? What kind of dog is that you have, Ted?" he asked. Ted replied, "Just an old alley dog."

Ted and Joe had learned how to hunt rabbits in snow. They liked hunting on that pretty white snow. After the sun had shone on it for three days with temperatures reaching high as thirty-six degrees, the snow would melt just enough to make it nice to walk on. The rabbits had left the fields and woods. Some went into holes, some moved into muck patches, and others would find green trees and bush. And that's where they would stay until the snow melted. The larger the area was, the more the rabbits would go to it. They had their own little roads they traveled in under the bushes. The dogs would run rabbits all day long in a large area. The bushes were tall enough for the dogs to go under without knocking the snow off. The rabbit trails were large enough for dogs to travel. It was hard to shoot one in this type of place. There were open spots between some of the bushes.

Twelve to twenty inches, the hunters would say, "Here he is," "There he goes," "He's coming your way."

There were lots of places like this in Oakland County. All the hunters had to do was to find them. Ted had taken time out and found himself some good spots to hunt. There was one place that he liked the best in Ortonville, on Grange Hill Road, one mile east of Dixie Highway. It was on the south side of the road between two large hills. It was a wonderful sight. At the bottom, it seemed as though all the rabbits in this area came to this spot. Most of the small bushes were only two to three feet high. Snow was one feet deep on level ground, and in some places, it drifted two feet or more.

Whenever he had taken Joe to this place and let him out of the car, he would go through the snow until he reached this place. When Ted put his boots and jacket on, he would be tracking straight away. Ted never got in a hurry because he knew that the rabbits had made trails under those bushes.

The rabbits would run up and down those trails for hours. Then he would start crawling through the large bunches of evergreens, making it hard on Joe to keep on tracking. It did slow him down, but he never stopped. Ted would walk out in the area where the bushes were small and not so thick. There he would wait for a rabbit to come hopping along the trail, going to where there were more and more large bushes. This way he would have a chance to kill him. When the other hunters found out about this, they came with many dogs and friends, killed and chased most of the rabbits away. Now Ted hated that he had taken his friends to this place. He no longer could go to this place, kill four rabbits in four hours, and go home. Ted called this place Rabbit City. They ate the leaves off those bushes and ate snow for water. They did not have to leave this place until the snow had melted.

The rabbits in cornfields, bean fields, and other fields would go into holes when snow was on the ground. The state had some men that planted fields of corn for the game to eat; they would plant a place in the field with running rosebushes with stickers on them; it would be about six feet wide. This was for the game protection. It would run the full length of the field; the larger the field, the more they would plant. Joe was too large to crawl around under the briars. The men could not walk through them; only the small beagles were able to crawl under them. These places would save lots of rabbits' lives. Joe hated these briars. When the small dogs were tracking in the rosebushes, he would run along one side barking. Most of the time the rabbits would go out on the opposite side; then Joe would have to find him a crossing place. After he crossed, he would take over. He's the main tracking dog now. Ted would listen for Joe's bark. Whenever he heard him, he knew that the rabbit was not far in front of him. When the rabbit was a long way ahead of him, he would not bark on his trail. He would trail him silently until he got closer to him, then he would start barking. Ted would walk across the field of woods and get in front of him, if he moved early enough. All he's have to do is wait for the rabbit, then he would be able to kill him.

Ted had become the number one hunter. Among the other hunters, he always killed the most game. Jack would always say, "Ted is lucky all the game comes directly to him. He could kill them with the barrel of his gun. He wasted shells when he shot them."

Ted looked at him and laughed. Then he said, "You know who the best hunter is?" Everyone was at a loss for words. Even ol' loudmouth didn't have much to say.

Jack said, "Men, Ted thinks that he's somebody with that ol' big-headed dog of his." Ted bought a female beagle puppy to hunt with Joe; she started hunting at the age of six months old. She was small enough to crawl under the rosebushes and brush piles that Joe could not go under. They made a good team. When those two dogs got on a trail, that little fellow had to find a hole in the ground or a brush pile that Dot could not enter.

They were good, and Ted knew it. All Jack would say was, "Boy, you made a real dog out of Joe. I would have betted my last dime that he would never make a good hunting dog. It's too bad that old Ben is dead. I wish that I could hunt those two together just to see which one is the best."

Ted replied, "I am glad that he is not here. If he was alive, when Joe got through with him, you would shoot him yourself for hunting so bad."

Jack uttered softly with tears in his eyes, "You know that Ben was the best dog around here." Ted looked at him, feeling sorry for him; then, he said, "I will have to admit it. He was good." They sat in the backyard and talked about the good times.

After Jack lost Ben, he tried to find another dog that could hunt like he did. He looked here and there, trying to find a good tracking dog. He did find one that was good; he called him Head because he had a large head for his body! Jack just knew that he had another *Ben*. He started bragging about Head before he got to the woods. All the hunters were looking forward to seeing Head run rabbits. The first two rabbits that the dog ran that day, Head had led the pack most of the time. Jack was bragging when the third rabbit got up. All the dogs ran him except Head. He came back to Jack and followed him the rest of the day. Jack did not give any one else a chance to talk. He talked and fussed at Head the rest of the day. Jack killed less rabbits than anyone else that day; they felt sorry, sorry for old loudmouth. They told him not to worry. Head was tired he would do better the next time. Jack said, "He only ran two rabbits, how could he be tired!" Ted spoke, "He will do better the next time. He has to get used to the other dogs." Jack said, "That's all right. You guys can say anything you want to 'cause I know better. Look at old Joe. He hunted better than that when he just learned to hunt." They all told him that his dog would do better the next time. Just before the season was over, Jack said, "I will not be hunting with you guys anymore. I *am* going back to school and become a barber. I will give Head to anyone who wants him.

He might hunt for someone else." This was sad news to the other hunters; they were looking forward to hunting with him because he was the life of the party. Jack was a good hunter and shooter. He shot his rabbit from many positions: standing up, squatting down, on his knees, and lying flat on the ground on his stomach. He was the only one in that group that could shoot that way.

Chapter 2

Joe is good; Ted knew that. He must take him back home to show those boys what a good hunting dog Joe was. Three years had passed when Joe had become the number one tracking dog.

All those fast dogs the boys were bragging on because they track fast, for a while. Soon they lost the track. That was when Joe took over and showed those hunters what old Hollering Boy could do. The whole group of men that hunted with Joe claimed him, never giving Ted the credit. That was all right with Ted. Jack no longer said he was tracking.

Hunting season had opened. It was in the month of November. Ted went home for Thanksgiving. The weather was nice, not hot, not cold, but just right for hunting. The sun was shining bright. There was just a breeze in this one Thanksgiving Day. Some of his friends and his brother went hunting with him. They also brought their dogs with them. Their dogs were larger than Joe.

Their sizes did not stop Joe from hunting. He had a job to do, and that is what he'll do. They hunted the farm that Ted was raised on and some of the other farms that were nearby. They stopped hunting at 2:00 p.m. and went to Ted's father's house where they all ate dinner. After dinner, they rested for one hour, then they went back out to hunt some more. They hunted three more hours, then, they quit and went back to the house.

They put leashes on their dog so they would not keep on hunting. They cleaned their game; then they sat around talking and drinking coffee. Some of them were drinking stronger drinks and discussing where they were going to hunt that Friday. Ted told them that he would take them to his uncle Ted's farm where they can hunt all day long. He said he knew that lots of rabbits were on his farm.

The second day, Ted had taken them up to his uncle's place, the one that he was named after. That morning, they hunted at the field across the road in front of his house. They came in for lunch; Ted had to tie Joe up because he did not want to stop hunting. There they had fried rabbit, collard greens, black-eyed peas, corn bread, and apple pie. Everyone enjoyed the dinner that Ted and Aunt Sarah had cooked. After they had rested for an hour, they hunted in the field behind the house and in the cow pasture. Boy, oh boy, the rabbits were running all around the place. Every hunter was having fun shooting their guns. All the men did their share of shooting. It was getting late in the evening. The dogs had hunted well. The men were getting tired. The dogs were tracking a rabbit; he left the field and went into the cow pasture, over a small hill in the muck patch. The dogs soon lost his track; they came out and sat on the hillside, except for Joe. He kept on hunting and barking at least over two minutes. Some of the hunters sat on old tree stumps, some on trees that had fallen down to the ground, and some on large rocks. Everybody was waiting and watching for Joe to find the rabbit.

Walter Jackson stopped at top of the hill, in the cow's path. A tree had fallen across the cow's path; he had taken himself a seat in the middle of the path. Walter said, "Let's go home, the dogs are tired." Ted said, "Give the old man a chance."

Joe was still tracking. He trailed the rabbit to the far end of the muck patch. The rabbit came out and got into the cow's path that went by the end of the muck patch. The rabbit headed straight for Walter and Joe right behind him. Walter started hollering, "Get back, get back," with a loud voice and waving his gun.

The rabbit and Joe kept coming. The rabbit ran up to him and jumped over his head. Joe went around him. He jumped up. Walter gun went *boom, boom!* He missed him. He cried out. Now all the dogs were barking. Oh boy, they were singing a natural song like the hunters like to hear. Soon the men were around Walter, asking him why he was hollering.

Walter cried with a loud voice, "That crazy old dog of Ted's ran that rabbit until he went crazy. That rabbit came up that trail straight for me. I could not make him turn. I threw up my hands and my gun. He never stopped coming. He ran up to me and leaped over my head, large as I am, you know that he had to see me. I turned and shot at him twice, but I missed him. That crazy old dog was right behind him."

While the hunters were checking on Walter, they forgot about the dog and the rabbit. All the dogs had stopped barking. The hunters started hollering to the dogs. The dogs would not bark. Some of them said they had lost him again. Ted listened for a while; then he said something was wrong. Joe had stopped barking. The hunters got together and went looking for the dogs. They found them one by one. Those dogs were large dogs; some were bluetick. The others were redbone hounds. The last two they found were eating the rabbit; they had torn the rabbit in two pieces. Joe was no match against those dogs. Joe came to Ted. Ted patted him on the head and said, "Good boy." Then Ted said to the other hunters, "Let's go home." We have had enough fun for one day. Walter said, "You are right. You can take that old crazy dog of yours back to Michigan."

Ted said, "Don't worry, he is going back with me. You hunters don't know how to appreciate a good dog when you see one." Walter said, "The dog is crazy. He doesn't know how to stop hunting." Ted replied, "He's not crazy. He's good. He doesn't lose a rabbit fast. He will not bark at a hole if the rabbit goes in it. I mostly kill everyone he tracks. Tomorrow we are going home. There he will hunt with dogs his own size, then he will be the king of the woods." When they got back home, Joe was ready.

Chapter 3

Ted's nephew, James Woods, that lived with him, was fourteen years old. He wanted to hunt too. Ted got a four-ten shotgun for him to hunt with. His gun was smaller than the other hunters, also lighter. Ted taught him how to hunt with it. After he had learned how to hunt well, he asked Ted to make a deal with him. The one that killed the less game would have to clean all the game. This sounds good to Ted. He said that it was a good deal. James did not know how good his uncle could shoot.

They went hunting. Ted would give him a chance to kill the first rabbit. Then, his uncle would say to him, "You got to kill every rabbit before I get a chance to shoot."

One day J. B., James, and Ted went hunting together. JB had grown himself a beard. The men called him Goatbeard. Joe and Dot were really running rabbits that day. James had killed six rabbits; Ted had killed the same amount. Goatbeard had done lots of shooting and killed nothing. The dogs were running the rabbits. They went out of hearing distance. Twenty minutes later, they heard them coming back. The rabbits came by James.

He would not shoot at him. Then, he passed by Goatbeard, and his gun went *boom! boom!* Then he hollered, "He's coming your way, Ted." Ted waited for the rabbit to come pass; then he raised his gun, aimed it, pulled the trigger, and killed him. So they headed for home after they had taken Goatbeard home.

James said, "Uncle, I could have beaten you today. I could have killed that last rabbit that you killed. I let him pass by me. I wanted

Goatbeard to kill him because he hadn't killed anything all day. He shot at him twice and missed both times. He was headed your way, and I knew then that you were going to kill him."

Ted replied, "You are a good sport. Don't worry I will clean the game today."

Monday night when Ted went to work at 11:00 p.m., after he had worked for two hours, he went over and talked with Goatbeard. Goatbeard said, "That boy James was shooting. He killed a rabbit that I missed. Man, that rabbit was really running. He only shot one time, and he rolled him like a ball. I got to admit, he made me look bad."

Ted said, "Don't worry. You got to get used to your new gun. You were hunting with that old crooked barrel gun so long. You will have to learn how to shoot a straight-barrel gun."

"Oh!" Goatbeard laughed. "Haw haw!" Then he said, "I hunted with that gun for years before I found out that the barrel was bent." The talk Ted had with Goatbeard cheered him up. He forgot about himself. He began to talk about Joe and Dot. Those dogs ran some rabbits that day, never losing one. Ol' Hollering Boy was good, Ted knew it. Dot did a lot of barking. Goatbeard thought she was the best. Ted did not care what he thought. He knew which one was the best. He never tried to prove it. One day they would find it out for themselves.

Now was the time for Ted to let Goatbeard find out how good Joe was. After they got off work, Ted went home, fixed his breakfast, changed clothes, put on his hunting suit and boots. Then he took his gun and shells, put them in the car, went to the dog pen, took Joe out, put him in the car, got in the car, went by and picked up Goatbeard, and drove to one of his favorite hunting places in Oakland County. He parked the car, opened the trunk, and let the dogs out.

Goatbeard yelled, "Where is the other dog?" Ted replied, "I left her in the dog pen." "What is wrong with her?" he asked. Ted looked at him and spoke softly, "Nothing." He looked at Ted with a frown on his face, then he said, "I should shoot you in your black ass for bringing me out here with the worst dog you have. We are not going to catch shit today. Let's go back home." Ted said, "Don't worry, we will catch some rabbits today."

With that, he shouted. Ted laughed, "Haw haw!" Then he spoke softly, "Come, we've got some hunting to do."

Ted went to a hunting area where there were less briars. Joe could run the rabbits until someone killed it or it went into a hole. As they walked through the brown grass, Goatbeard was walking and talking in front of him. His gun went *boom! boom!*

Ted hollered, "Did you get him?" He said, "Naw." "Call the dog and put him on his track," Ted hollered.

He called Joe and pointed to the ground in the direction he went, and soon Joe picked up his scent through the grass, and he went barking at a slow pace.

Goatbeard said, "That is one rabbit we can forget about." Ted spoke, "Stay where you are and don't move. He will bring the rabbit back to you." Soon the rabbit came hopping back. Goatbeard was standing there waiting. His gun went boom! He hollered, "I got him." "Here, Joe, here, Joe," he called. Joe came. He let him smell the rabbit, put him in his game bag, patted Joe on the head, and said, "Goody boy. Good boy."

He yelled, "Ted, I am ready to hunt now," calling Joe as he walked through the grass. Soon Joe was trailing another rabbit. In five hours, they had jumped six rabbits and killed them all. Now it was time for them to go home; they had to get some sleep before they went to work.

On their way home, Goatbeard said, "We jumped six rabbits. We killed them all. We could have killed lots of rabbits today."

Ted said, "When Joe hunts by himself, he'll bark just enough to let you know which way he's going. When the rabbits don't run fast, they're easier to shoot. When Dot is with him, she does most of the barking. Joe will not bark on a cold track or at a hole. Dot loves to bark. She will bark when the track is cold or hot. You will have to take her away from a hole." He said, "Let me tell you something. Don't bring Dot anymore. Old Joe is all we need."

Goatbeard was happy as they went home. That night at work, when he caught up on his job, he came over and talked with Ted. He said, "I am glad that you did not bring Dot. That Joe is some dog. I did not know that he was that good." Ted replied, "Both of them are good. They will run their own rabbit. They don't need any help." He said, "I don't care how many times we go hunting, please don't bring Dot. Joe is the dog I want to hunt with." Ted looked at him, smiled, then he said, "I thought you didn't want to hunt unless Dot was with us." He spoke, "Man, I did say that. I need my ass kicked. I didn't know that Joe was so good." Ted uttered, "If you want to know which one was the best, you should have asked me." "I thought that I could tell which one was the best by listening to them track rabbits," Goatbeard said. They talked for thirty minutes. Just before he left, he asked Ted, "When are we going back out?" Ted told him that he would not be able to go out for a while. Goatbeard asked Ted to let him take Joe hunting Saturday.

"I want to take my older boy hunting, and I want him to see Joe hunt," Goatbeard said. Ted told him that Chuck wanted to take Dot and Joe hunting with him. "I will tell Chuck to leave Joe for you." That Saturday, Chuck came and took Dot. Goatbeard came and got Joe. Oh what a day he had. The next week, every day, he would come over to Ted's job and tell him about the fun they had with Joe and how his boy enjoyed the hunt. He told his hunting friends about Joe. He talked so much about the dog until they wanted to hunt with him. This made Ted proud of Joe. He was a dog that he could depend on.

Many years had passed. The game was scarce, and the hunting bunch had drifted apart. They all hunted with Joe whenever Ted and Chuck would let them. Two things happened to Joe that had made him a slow tracker. One was that someone broke his right hind leg below the knee. Ted had taken him to the doctor. The doctor fixed it. The other thing was that he had crawled over and through a fence, got hung up, and hurt his back. For six months he couldn't use his hind legs, and back to the doctor he went. Ted did not mind paying his doctor's bill. To Ted, he was worth his weight in gold. It was about six months before Joe was able to walk again.

When he walked, his back end wobbled. This did not stop him from hunting. He always wanted to go with Ted. He took him as the years passed. Joe grew stronger and stronger. He never grew strong enough to be the lead dog again though. After years had passed by, Joe's nickname had been changed from Pretty Boy or Hollering Boy to the Old Man. All of the other dogs outtracked him. That was all right with Ted. They would lose the track. Whenever they went hunting, the boys wanted to take the old man, not because he was a fast tracker. They wanted him because he was a good tracker dog. When the other dogs lost the track and stopped hunting, the old man would take over. He was always there to straighten it out. If a new man was hunting with them, the other hunter would ask him to stand still and watch the old man do his job. Some of the men had bought registered beagles. Joe made them all look bad.

All the hunters stood still, waiting and watching the old man do what he did best. The men placed themselves around the swamp like a horseshoe is made. The rabbits had only one way to get out alive, and that is to go back up the swamp. Now it was left up to the rabbit which way he would run. The old man said he got to make his move soon. The hunters are waiting for him to come out. The other dog was back up the swamp trying to get the track straight.

One day, they took Ted and Joe out with one of the guys that they bought their dogs from. This man bragged about his dogs.

Ted said to him, "Papers don't make a dog. You have to train them." As they hunted that day, his dogs were good. They were fast. It looked like Joe would not get a chance to show them what he could do. Ten rabbits were jumped and killed. The eleventh rabbit did some running. Those dogs were tracking good. This rabbit ran for forty-five minutes before he decided to trick those dogs. He left the woods and came up in the field about three hundred feet away, turned around, and went right back the same way he had come. When he had reached the swamp, he turned right, went about twenty feet, and stopped cold. They did not know what to do.

Now the time had come for the old man to show those young dogs something.

Roger Spand said, "You all can call your dogs in. They will never find that rabbit." Ted spoke softly, as they stood in the field, "Wait for the old man to say that he can't be found. Then I will be ready to go." Roger said, "I have never seen a dog that could track as well as my dog does." Ted spoke in a loud voice, "Let's wait until the old man says the rabbit can't be found, then I will be satisfied." Chuck yelled, "You heard the man, we will wait, and see what happens." He knew that Joe would find the rabbit. This would be a good way for him to stop Roger from bragging about a registered dog. It's good to have papers on your dog, but papers don't train a dog. A man has to work hard when training a dog. He can't be trained overnight. Chuck knew that.

When he went back to work, Roger would wish that he had never gone hunting with Ted and that old broken-down dog. Joe was going to find that rabbit. Chuck was going to laugh and tell the news to the men that he worked with.

Joe was tracking that rabbit behind all those good dogs. Some were sitting down by their masters; the others were running around in the field.

Joe was working hard to bring up the rear. Chuck was standing there with a big grin on his face as the old man came hopping and straggling out of the small swamp into the field like a drunken man.

Roger looked at him and said, "Men, we are wasting our time. We could have jumped at least two more rabbits and killed them by now. Here we are waiting on a dog that can hardly run, let alone catch rabbits."

Joe went to the field where the other dogs had stopped tracking. He went to the right. He came back and went to the left; then he made a large circle. He couldn't pick up the track. He came back to the trail, raised his head in the air howling, looking at the men. Ted said, "Find him, boy." He turned around and went back the same way that he had come from. Roger hollered, "Look, look, that dog is backtracking. We all saw him come up the same way. He's going back. Call your dogs, men, before that dog has all of them backtracking."

Ted said, "My dog will not backtrack. Keep looking at him. He is going off to your right. He did not come that way out of the swamp."

Roger uttered, "We'll see what's going to happen." Joe went back into the swamp, barking once every two minutes. He went about twenty-five feet in the swamp, then started going around in a circle. All at once he started barking like he was looking at the rabbit. Ted yelled, "Catch him, Joe." Then he laughed. All at once, he stopped and cried out, "He is going up the swamp." Roger went across the field to the edge of the swamp to Ted's right side. They were headed up the swamp. Every dog that was there, ran into the woods where Joe was. Now the hunt was on. Those fast dogs were back on the job. For fifteen minutes, they ran that rabbit. Soon Roger saw him. He raised his gun putting the stock to his shoulder, pointing the barrel at the rabbit, taking aim, then he pulled the trigger. He hit that rabbit. The rabbit ran about fifty feet and died. Those fast dogs ran so fast they ran over him and did not know it. The old man came along and found him, picked him up as usual. Roger's main dog saw him, came over, and grabbed hold. They were pulling on the rabbit. Ted could not hear the old man. He hollered to Roger and asked him if he killed the rabbit.

He replied, "*No*, I hit him. He was too far from me to kill." Ted said, "Where is Joe? When you find him, you will find your rabbit." Roger hollered back, "I see all the dogs but Joe, and one of mine." Ted asked him to keep looking. He said, "When you find them, you will find your rabbit." Roger went in the woods, going the way he saw the rabbit go.

Soon he heard the dogs growling at one another. He walked over to them and yelled back with a loud voice, "I found them, they have the rabbit." Ted hollered, "Make your dog turn him loose, before they tear him apart. Don't try to take him from Joe. He will bring him to me, and I will give him to you."

Roger did just what Ted asked him to do. Joe laid the rabbit down and growled at Roger. Roger hollered, "He has laid the rabbit down, and now he's growling at me." Ted replied, "Don't bother him. Walk away." Then he yelled, "Joe, bring me the rabbit."

Joe picked up the rabbit and headed for Ted. As he walked out of the woods with the rabbit hanging out of his mouth, he headed straight for Ted. As all the men stood there watching, Chuck yelled, "Men, that's a number one rabbit dog. Take a good look at him."

Roger asked, "Are you sure that's not a registered dog?" Ted said, "I'm sure. I got him from the dog pound for ten dollars, and he didn't know how to hunt. I trained him, myself." Roger said, "I got to admit, he's good." Chuck said, "Why are we standing around here talking, I came out here to hunt." Roger said, "I've got to go." Chuck asked, "What's wrong? Are you afraid that Joe is going to teach your dogs how to track?" "He is good," Roger admitted. "The best I've ever hunted with. My dogs could learn from him. He has to be a registered dog. No mongrel can hunt like that. He hunts from the heart. Boys, I hate to say this, but I have to go home." Ted spoke, "We have had enough fun for one day."

They all called their dogs in, put them in the trunk of their cars, made sure that every man had a rabbit to take home. The one that didn't kill one still got one from the man that had killed the most. They traveled home. The men that rode with Ted began to talk about what Joe did to those other dogs. One of them said, "Ted, why did you do us that way? We could have taken the dogs and hunted in another place while Joe was looking for the rabbit they lost. You know that he was not going to stop until he found him. You just had to show Roger's dog up."

Ted laughed, then he said, "I wanted all of you to see with your own eyes, how good the old man is. Most of the hunters that were with us had hunted with him before he got hurt. Some of you didn't want to go hunting without him. Now all the other hunters are going crazy over a dog with a piece of paper. All of those dogs with a good bloodline. Let the old man show the up. I trained him. I've seen him find rabbits in a swamp. Those four men had hunted with their dogs for three and a half hours. They had only seen one rabbit. Their dogs were not able to track him. Before I reached the swamp, my dogs were running a rabbit. After I had killed two rabbits, they were still standing. I asked them to come and hunt with us. In two hours, we had jumped fourteen rabbits and killed all but two. Those two went into a hole in the ground. After that we went home. I know what the old man can do, and what he's been through."

No one else said a word about the old man. Soon they were at home. Ted backed his car into the driveway, opened the trunk, and left it open for Joe to get out.

After he stood up in the trunk and walked to the edge, Ted would go and take him out, and if he tried to pick him up before he stood up, he would bite.

The weekend soon passed. It was work time again. That Monday, Chuck told the men on the job about Roger's good dogs that he had been bragging on and how a crossbred dog ran Roger and his dogs out of the woods, Saturday. Roger did not have anything to say. He sent word by Chuck to Ted that he would let him have both of his dogs for seventy dollars. He was going to quit hunting.

When Ted heard the news, he felt real bad. He knew that Roger's dogs were young and inexperienced. As the years passed and he kept on hunting them, they'd learn more about tracking rabbits. They were too good for the price that he was asking. One of them is worth more than that price. He didn't need another dog. He turned to Chuck and asked him, "What did you do to Roger to make him give his dogs away?" Chuck replied, "I told the boys on the job about those dogs. I closed his mouth for good." Ted replied, "I want you to tell Roger to keep his dogs, train them once a week, and let them track that rabbit until they catch it. When they lose the trail, take them back to where they lost it. Encourage them to find him. This will make them better. If he lives close by the woods, train them in it. After he got them used to hunting there, he can turn them loose, and they will go to the woods on their own, every time they get loose."

Chuck took this information back to Roger. Roger's response was, "I have quit hunting. I no longer need the dogs. This is why I'm getting rid of them. I would like for Ted to take them and hunt them with his old dog. With what they know and what he would teach them, soon they would be as good as Joe." When Chuck told

Ted what Roger had said, Ted replied, "Rabbits are getting scarce. Soon I too will quit hunting them. When the old man get to old to hunt, I too am quitting. You take the dogs."

Chuck spoke, "No, no, I have two young dogs that have started hunting. I don't want them hunting with any other dogs but Joe. After he teaches them all about tracking, then I will hunt them with other dogs."

As the years passed, Chuck's dogs were running good. Rabbits were getting scarcer and scarcer. Ted could not go with them because of his job. Chuck carried the old man with him; he also hunted in Canada, Ohio, Indiana, Tennessee, and Kentucky. He would come back and brag to Ted about how he killed more rabbits than the other men. He always took the old man with him. Whenever the old man started barking, he would make his way close to him. Those young dogs of his stayed right with the old man.

One day after hunting season was closed, Jack came to Ted and asked him, "Will you teach me how to train a young dog how to hunt like you have Joe hunting? Do not think I am trying to be funny. My dog is good. He has a habit that I cannot break him from. After he tracks two rabbits, he will quit hunting. All the other dogs keep on hunting until we get ready to quit and come home. I used to kid you about Joe. I got to admit he had made me and my dog look bad. When you refuse to go hunting with us, the boys tell me to leave my dog at home and ask you to let me carry Joe."

Ted said, "You can carry Joe hunting with you whenever you want to." Ted was willing to share Joe with his hunting buddies.

Jack went to the dog pound trying to find himself a young dog that he could train. He kept on going until he found an old dog that was already trained. Out of all the dogs they had, they still wanted Joe.

Ted was a good-hearted man. He said to them, "You all can carry Joe hunting whenever Jack and I are not going hunting."

Everything was going fine for a while. Soon rabbits became hard to find. The hunters started going farther and farther away. Ted and Jack stopped going hunting with them. They would come by and get Joe. Soon the hunters split up and started hunting in different places and states. All of them wanted to take Joe with them. Ted said that the one that asked him first get to take Joe with him. That worked good for a while. Chuck lived closer to Ted than the rest of the hunters. He was asking first. Some of the fellows became angry whenever they asked Ted about taking Joe hunting and he told them Chuck was taking him. Bob came by early in the morning and got Joe. When Chuck arrived, they had taken Joe away. Ted did not get off work until 7:00 a.m. When he got home, the hunters would be in the fields hunting. Chuck was hunting that day with malice in his heart thinking Ted let someone else have Joe. His mind was made up about what he was going to tell Ted. When he knocked on Ted's door, Ted opened the door and said, "Hi, Chuck, I know you had lots of fun today."

Chuck answered, "How could I? Why you did not let me have Joe?" Ted replied, "I thought you came and got him this morning." Chuck said, "I came, but Joe was not here. Who did you let take Joe?"

Ted said, "Bob asked me about taking Joe hunting with him. I told him you were taking Joe with you."

Chuck laughed, then said that he knew who came by and got Joe. "I know it. I know it. The last time we were out together, I killed the most rabbits. I gave some of the fellow rabbits that did not kill any rabbits. I also told him why I was able to kill the most rabbits."

Then he turned and looked at Ted and said, "You are the cause of this." Ted screamed at him, "I told you not to tell anyone about our secret that we have learned about Joe. Joe is not the fastest dog nor the slowest one. He has become the only one you can depend on when the other dogs have given up on the rabbit trail and lost his trail and quit. That is when Joe steps in, takes over, and finds that rabbit. He stops barking like the rest of the dogs, but he keeps on looking for that rabbit until he finds his or her trail. Then when he does bark, he would be in a different spot. He is letting you know that the rabbit is still running. The other dogs would be trying to find them another rabbit to run.

"The rabbit knows he has the dogs. Now he will run a little piece, stop, stand on his back legs and look back for the dogs. He cannot see or hear but one dog on his track. He will lick his two front feet, then he will make one long leap to the right side or the left side. He or she will hop in a tall bunch of grass where his feet touch the ground. He or she will sit there.

"When the dogs come down the trail to where the rabbit stops, they will stop tracking. That rabbit thinks he has fooled Joe like he did the other dogs. Joe has reached the end of that rabbit's trail. He went forth twenty feet. He could not smell the rabbit track. He made a circle about twenty feet on the right side of the trail. Then he did the same thing on the left side. He kept on making those circles. Each one came closer. I hollered, 'Just look at the old man work. Now, that is a rabbit dog.' Soon he found where that rabbit was sitting. He could smell his scent on the grass. He can't sit there any longer. He got to move because Joe wants him for lunch.

"The noise that Joe was making made the other dogs come running to help him. It was too late. George killed the rabbit when he was passing by.

"I told him about how Joe caught a rabbit, hold him down with his two front feet, turn him on his back, and pull hair off his stomach. He got off the rabbit and shook the fur out of his mouth. The rabbit took off running. He took off behind him, caught the rabbit again, and did the same thing. He took his feet off the rabbit to get the fur out of his mouth. The rabbit took off running, with

Joe right behind him. He caught him and did the same to him. As the rabbit was passing by me, I reached down and picked him up. That rabbit was so tired he could hardly run. That was the first dog I have seen that did not know how to kill a rabbit."

Ted asked, "Why did you tell all those stories about Joe?" Chuck said, "Man, I had to tell someone about how good Joe is. Those guys running around bragging on their dogs because they have a loud voice. Some can track fast, but when the rabbit makes a few turns, they lose the rabbit track. That is when Joe takes over. That is what my dog does."

Ted laughed, then said, "I thought he was my dog." Chuck replied, "I suppose he is your dog. I have got used to telling people he was my dog. Let me tell you something about your dog. Whenever he gets out of his pen, he will come over to my house and lay down on the porch. He will not allow anyone to come upon the porch. My wife and children have to use the back door. He did bite my oldest when he tried to make him get off the porch. From then on, no one bothered him whenever he comes over.

"When I come home and see him sitting on my front porch, I am so glad. I know what he wants. He wants someone to take him hunting.

"Ted, let me tell you something about Joe. I let him stay in the house. Sometimes I put him a pallet on the floor in the living room. As long as I am awake, walking around in the house, he will stay on it. When I go to bed, he will come and lie in front of the door. He will not let anyone in the room where I am, not even my wife.

"She always cooks an extra piece of meat just for him. She will call him, show him the meat, open the back door, and throw it in the yard. Out the door he will go. Now, she can come in the room with me. Joe does so many things. I really can't tell you all the things he will do."

Ted replied, "You are right. No one knows how good a tracker he is or what he will do next. He can track on ice and snow."

"Once more, I get to shoot Bob if I had Joe," Chuck said.

Ted said, "You will not shoot anyone. We all are friends. The most important part is we are hunting buddies. I gave six of you all, puppies of Joe's. I trained them myself. I know that they track a rabbit like their father. Now tell me what happen to the one you had."

Chuck replied, "My wife's brother shot him for a rabbit in some tall grass. That puppy could really track a rabbit. If he had not been my brother-in-law, I would have shot him."

Ted said, "Out of all those puppies I raised and trained and let you all have them, only one is still alive. That's the one Sam has. He is good. Sam changed his name from Hard Rock to Prince. He said his father is the king. He is next to his father or better. Rev. King took his puppy to his sister. Somehow he made them gun shy. I know what happened to the other two. I will say this only once to you. I will let you keep Joe if you promise to stop talking about shooting Bob."

Chuck said, "Man, I was only kidding with you. I would not shoot anyone. I got my family to think about."

"You promise me you will take care of Joe. One day, I will be able to go hunting with you all. Again, where we use to hunt, it is hard to find a rabbit. It's no fun in walking all day and not finding anything to shoot," Ted said.

The hunters were going from state to state looking for rabbits. They went to Canada, where there were lots of rabbits.

Ted said, "Come by Sunday evening and take him with you. Take care of him. He is the last rabbit dog I will train."

When hunting season was over, Chuck kept on training his dogs. He would say one day that they'd track just like Joe. Every hunter has a certain place where he trains his dogs. There was a field and woods behind the state police station on Telegraph Road, north of the Pontiac Mall. He would park his car close to the swamp, turn his dogs loose, and let them hunt. While they were tracking, he sat in the car and listened. He took them out one Wednesday evening. They were trailing a rabbit. He was enjoying listening to them. Soon they quit barking.

He waited fifteen minutes for them to start barking again. The female dog came back to him. Now he was worried. He called and called. He could not hear them, and they wouldn't come. He walked through the woods where he heard them last. First he thought that Joe had a heart attack because of his age. He looked and looked. He couldn't see nor hear them anywhere. Now he was getting worried. He came and got Ted, telling him what had happened. They both went back to the swamp and looked for the dogs.

Soon Ted said, "Someone must have taken those dogs." Chuck spoke, "No one has come out or in by me. People live on the other side and at the end of this swamp. How would they catch them anyway?" Ted replied, "They took a female that's in heat, walked across in front of your dogs. Those dogs, the male ones, will take off behind her. We can forget about those dogs."

Chuck replied, "No way, I will run an ad in the paper offering a reward." Ted looked at Chuck and spoke softly, "Those dogs are good. No way will you get them back." Chuck uttered with tears in his eyes, "Those dogs are good. Little boys are good, almost as good as Joe. I am coming back out here every day to listen to see if I hear them bark. I am going to get my dogs if I hear them."

Ted said, "Don't worry, we had the best. He will never be forgotten by the men that hunted with him." Chuck shed tears. They never found those dogs. Sometimes Ted met with new hunters as they talked about hunting and their dogs. Ted would speak of Joe.

There will be someone in the midst who would say that they went hunting with a man that had a dog named Joe. "Boy, that big-headed dog could track, even though he staggered when he walked." Ted would say sometimes it was his dog. Some of the hunters would say, "You mean to tell me that a dog that was that good, you let someone else take hunting?"

Ted said, "Yes! The more he hunted, the better he got. Hunting does not hurt a dog."

The memory of amazing Joe lives on.

Joe and Dot

Joe's Hunting Mate (Dot)

Here is true story you about two rabbits dog that Ted trained. It was in the fall of the year. Hunting season had opened up.

Ted and three of his friends went together and took the dogs hunting. When they reached the hunting area, some hunters were putting their dogs in their cars. Ted parked beside this hunter.

As they talked, he said that they had jumped some rabbits. It was so dry that the dogs cannot track them.

Ted asked him to show him where he jumped the last rabbit.

He replied, "About one hundred feet from here. You go across the field, and just before you get to the tall grass, it will be on your right side."

Ted's dogs were named Dot and Joe. Dot was the female, and Joe was the male dog.

As Ted walked across the field, the other hunter hollered to Ted, "You are close to the spot. Go over to your right a little farther." Ted took Joe and Dot over a little farther to his right. Soon Dot picked up the rabbit track. She was his lead track dog. Joe was the number one track dog. You take a good look at these dogs. Now the hunt was on. Those two dogs aiming the hunting area up.

The other hunters that were back in the woods had come out of the hunting field. They had stopped, asked the other hunter that told them where he jumped the last rabbit.

He told them, "This man came in here with two dogs that make our dogs look bad. When they killed the rabbit, his dog finds another."

He replied, "Those dogs really sound good." The other hunters parked their cars beside the road, got out of them, and stood beside them just to watch Ted's dogs hunt.

Ted stood close to the swamp with a twelve-gauge automatic. Every time a rabbit came by, he would shoot one time, go over pick the rabbit up, and put him in his game bag.

He looked back to the road and hollered loud, "Come on and hunt with us." Someone said, "Can we bring our dogs?" Ted replied, "Yes, as long as they will hunt and not fight my dogs."

They all came and joined the hunt. Boy, oh boy, did they have a good time hunting. The hunt was good. Ted made sure every man had at least two rabbits a piece.

All the hunters wanted to know where Ted got his dogs from. Ted said, "The one I have a leash on, I found him in the dog pound."

How to Train a Rabbit Dog

Rabbit dogs are easy to train. You take a puppy when six months old. If hunting season is open, go out on a farm or state land that is open. Find yourself a live rabbit and kill it, if you can. If you cannot, find a hunter that will kill a rabbit for you. You want one with all his fur on him. Also, his feet and head are freshly killed.

Take him home with you. Cut the head off, leaving most of his neck on the body. Take the fur off the neck. Take the rabbit and hold it against the fence, letting a small amount of the rabbit stick through the fence.

Soon the puppy will start eating on it. Then you take it from him. Lay it close to the fence where he can see it, but not reach it. Leave it there for half an hour. Take it back to the fence. Let him chew on the neck again, for ten minutes, take it from him. Tie a string around the rabbit and drag it from the same spot where he was chewing on the rabbit. You drag the rabbit around in your yard, not going over the same spot and hide it.

Turn the puppy out at the spot where he was trying to eat the rabbit. Let him pick up the scent. Keep doing the same thing over until he picks up the rabbit scent. Soon he will find where you hid the rabbit. Do this over and over, making the drag longer. When you become tired, cut a piece of the rabbit off and give it to him.

Take the intestines out of the rabbit, leave the fur on him, put him in a freezer bag, put him in the freezer. When you want to make another drag, take him out, let him defrost. Then you make a long drag. When you have dragged until you are tired, pull the fur off the rabbit, cut him up, and give to your puppies.

You get another rabbit and do the same thing all over. Make the drags longer. After he or she has gotten good on tracking the drag, you can take them to a place where you will be able to find some wild live rabbits. Where no one is hunting. You want them to do all the tracking by themselves, no help from another dog.

When they are tracking and the rabbit come out of the tall grass close by you, you call them to you and hold your hand close to the ground, walking the way the rabbit went. Soon, they will pick up his scent. You are helping them to depend on you. When you call him to put on a rabbit trail, you call different from the way you call him when you want to catch him.

You call him by his name with your head turned away from you. Say, "Spot, here. Here, Spot here, here, here," moving in the way the rabbit went.

The more you hunt them, the better they will get. If you live close to a wooded area where you can turn them loose and let them hunt by themselves, that will be good for them.

Always check on them. Some people will take your dogs. Now you are teaching them how to depend on themselves and you. This way you will know what they are tracking. When you hunt them with another dog, ask the owner if his dogs hunt deer or foxes. If he says yes, do not let your dogs hunt with his dogs. If you do, you are taking a chance of losing your dogs. Once they start tracking deer, it's hard for you to catch up with your dog. Be sure that you put your nameplate on his collar, where someone can contact you if this happens.

This is the chance we hunters take. Some dogs have been found twenty-five miles from the place where they were hunting. When you are hunting in the daylight, you can get in your car and try to get in front of your dog before he gets out of your hearing. When you catch him, give him a whipping. Deers will cross fences and roads as fast as they get to them. If you catch him on a deer trail, put your leash on him and give him a whipping. If you hunt them three years by themselves, it will be hard for another dog to get them to track something else besides a rabbit. Don't quit training your dogs.

When hunting season is over, there is a training season in your game rule book that will tell you all about the training rules.

When you have followed these instructions of this little booklet and use it well, then you will know how good your dog is.

Rabbit Dog

Bluetick Coonhound

How to Train Coon Dogs At Six Months Old to Track Coons

This will not be easy. Your job is for you to find out which puppies will tree because his father and mother are good tree dogs.

Some of their puppies will not tree. Most of them will be good track dogs.

The best way for you to train them. You keep three coon hides in a freezer bag from last year's hunting season in your freezer. Take one out. Let it defrost. Tie a small rope to it. Throw it in your backyard with the puppies. Let them play with it while you hold one end of the rope.

At the age of three months old, you put a coon hide in the pen with them. Tie it to a fence post where they cannot take it into the doghouse.

If the weather is bad, leave it in the dog pen for two hours. Then, take it out and put it back into the freezer in a clean bag. Do this as often as you can.

Soon the puppies will start playing with it. Now they are doing what you want them to do. You tie a longer rope on the hide. Let them out in the backyard. Throw this hide out there where they are. When they pick up the hide and try to run with it, you pull on the rope. Soon when they will lose their hold, drag it a little way from them. They will catch up with it. You keep on doing this until they get real interested in that hide. You spend sometime in the yard playing with your puppies with the hide.

You throw that hide out in your yard like a fish reel, with your puppies, and pull it to you, slowly letting them catch a hold of it. Then you pull, pull on it, pulling it closer to you. You throw it back out in the yard, doing the same thing over and over, after you get them looking for you to throw that hide for them.

If your yard is large enough for you to make a short drag in it, you take the hide and lay it down at the gate and drag it around in the yard.

Go to a tree, dragging it up the tree about six feet, and tie it there. Go to the pen and let two of the puppies at a time out to pick up the track.

You do this day after day until they start following the drag. Now it is time for you to make a longer drag. You need to be sure when they bark at the tree, they can bark with their head straight up in the air. They will make good tree dogs. If you have one that will not bark with his head looking straight up the tree, that one will not make a good tree dog. He will make a good track dog. You will separate him from the other puppies when you make the drag. Let him or her track by himself or herself. This time you will have the coon hide hanging just out of his reach.

After you have tried and tried and he still won't tree, let someone have him for a fox hound or a rabbit dog.

When the other puppies get nine months old, you can take them coon hunting. Please do not let them get into a real coon fight. They are young and inexperienced. You can ruin them for life. Be sure that you have a dog that knows how to kill a coon.

I have seen one coon whip six dogs and walk away from them. When I no longer had a kill dog along with my dogs, I had a German shepherd that weighed 115 pounds. To me, he was worth his weight in gold.

He did no tracking when the other dogs treed the coons. He would be right there waiting for someone to knock him out of the tree. When the coon falls on the ground, he was always waiting to catch him. Once he caught him, he never let go until the coon was dead.

Sometimes the coon would catch a hold of him. First, he would shake him loose, walk backward, and go back in, and pick that coon up and shake him. The coons have lost the use of its back legs. I have to stop him before he kills the coon or the puppies get a chance to kill the coon.

Now the coon is lying flat on his back. He only has the use of his front legs and head. He is still dangerous. Your puppies have to learn how to kill that coon without that coon catching his head. Your puppies will go in for the kill, not knowing what that coon is going to do.

The first one to get close enough to his head is going to catch a hold of it and hold on to it. The other puppies will catch hold of the coon's body and pull on it. When that puppy gets loose, he will go back to the coon to kill him, if they are English blueticks. Most of the other breed of dogs will turn that coon on loose and bay him. That bluetick will keep going back until he kills him. You can have a good coon dog, but not a good kill dog. All dogs are not kill dogs.

When my bluetick puppies become one year old, I let two of them fight a coon one at a time. I would tie my other dog and let two puppies fight the coon when he is shot out of the tree.

When they become two years old, I will let one dog fight the coon. They would take a live coon and run through the woods together with him where they would kill the coon. They will leave him there. It is not easy to find a dead coon in the woods at night with a flashlight. That bluetick is good.

Now you know how to train your dogs. You want a dog with speed. You take a walker hound that trees coon and crossbreed it with a bluetick. Your puppies will be faster dogs on the track. Sometimes the fast dogs catch the coon before he gets to a tree. Some coons travel for a few miles looking for food. A coon cannot run as fast as a dog. Always have a male and female hunting together. This way your dogs will not fight each other at the tree. Those blueticks will fight at the tree. Some of them will try to climb the tree if the tree is leaning over against another tree. Some dogs will try to climb it behind the coon. Be sure all your dogs are standing at the bottom of the tree.

I had a friend that had a dog hunt for a coon this way. Now you take that redbone hound, he is good. To me the bluetick is the best.

Let's talk about the black-and-tan and old Smokie. He is a good track dog, a good tree dog, but not a good kill dog.

Let me tell you about my black-and-tan. He was good. One night, he treed up three trees at one time. The first tree had three coons in it. The second tree had eight half-grown coons in it. The third had one coon in it. I have never seen one dog tree that many coons at one time. I had two three-year-old dogs hunting with him and six puppies, nine months old. He left the two older dogs at the first tree. When he came to the second tree, it was an apple tree at the edge of the woods. He left all six of the puppies there. The old man kept on tracking by himself. There was still one coon on the ground running. After a while, he came to the largest trees in the woods. That is where he stopped and sat down and started barking. Now, this is the third tree that we have gone to. It is time for us to do our job. While we are trying to find the coon in this tree, Old Smokie leaves us looking for the coon while he goes from tree to tree, checking on the other dog. When he gets to the first tree, the old man opens up his mouth to let you know where he is. He went from tree to tree when he came back to us. We had found the coon. My buddy waited until Smokie had made his round, then he shot the coon out of the tree.

Now this dog had us speechless, sensing him going from tree to tree and the other dogs staying at their own tree.

Now we went to the apple tree where the puppies were, Smokie right with us. There we killed those coons. Now we went to the first tree. We killed those coons, now Smokie took off. We soon heard him doing his job.

We called him the old man because he was the oldest dog that we had. Also the most gentlest dog I had ever owned; even the puppies sleep with him and not their mother.

Now the dogs are hunting. Soon we had twelve coons in our hunting bag. The coons were heavy to carry. Now we head for the van. We called all the dogs in. Now we are trying to get to the van. Sometimes we were dragging the bag with the coons in it.

Our bags were made out of good material. It was a soldier's duffel bag. We were almost to the car; Old Smokie treed again.

We are tired and trying to go home. We cannot call him away from the tree. One of us got to go and got him. Since Ted was the oldest, he asked Don to go and get him. He had to go about half a mile before he came to the tree. He put his leash on Smokie. Then he looked up the tree with his flashlight. There he saw three coons up in the tree. Don called back to Ted and said, "It is three coons up this tree." Ted answered back, "Leave them there. We already have more than we want to carry." Smokie was the best black-and-tan dog that I had ever seen. We caught over one hundred coons that year.

Can I tell you a true story about Smokie? One night we went coon hunting as usual. Smokie picked up a coon trail. There was a lake of water close by. The coons went to the lake. Smokie was right behind them. They swam close to the edge of the lake for a while. We went over to the side of the lake where he was. No other dog would go in the water to help him.

Sometimes the coons would be chasing him. He headed straight for us. He goes about thirty feet from us. They turned around and went to a tree standing in the lake near the other side.

We called him, and we called him. When those coons saw us, they turned and went to the tree in the lake. He turned around and followed behind them.

We had our flashlight on them all the way in the water. Now they have reached the tree.

The first one went up the tree about five feet, stopped, turned around, and headed back down it.

The second one went up the tree about four feet and did the same thing. The third one went up the tree about two feet, stopped, and headed back down it.

Now this did not look good at all.

The closer the dog came to the tree, the coons came down the tree closer to the water. Now this did not look good for Smokie. He is not a kill dog.

If he swam up to that tree, that would be his last coon hunt. The water was too deep for his feet to reach the ground. Those coons were going to get a piggyback ride on his back.

A coon would kill the average dog in water. He would get on your dog's back, walk to his head, ride it under the water. When his rear end came up out of the water, he would walk the dog's back until he drowned him.

Smokie saw those coons on that tree. He turned around and swam to the bank where we were.

I put my leash on him. I thought that night those coons were going to kill my dog.

When I had English blueticks, no coon were able to make him turn and walk away.

A Coonhound Dog
Blue's And Ring's Last Hunt

In the year of 1976, Ben bought back one of the dogs that he had raised. His dog had nine puppies, and Ben kept two of the litter for himself. The rest he got rid of, including the mother. The father, he kept to train the two he had kept.

A year later, he got rid of the female because the neighbors complained about the dogs barking. He had to give the one away. This really hurt Ben because he knew that the father was growing old. It would be some time before the other dogs would be able to take his place. It's easy to catch young coons with young dogs because old coons will trick them every time. Ben knew that old dogs could not be replaced with young dogs.

That old bluetick was something, this Ben knew. It was hard for a coon to get away from him. Ben had never seen a coon make him back up in all the years he'd had him, nor had he ever seen him walk away from a fight, no matter how large the coon was.

Another year passed by, and Ben was proud of his young dog. That young dog hunted good with his father. Ben caught lots of coons. He caught coons when the other coon hunters that worked with him didn't.

The other hunters had been talking about Ben's dogs because they were not registered. They would sit down at work and talk about their dogs' bloodline and what their dog's grandparents did and the amount of money they paid for their dogs.

Ben laughed; then said, papers do not make a dog. They called Ben's dogs mongrels because they were not thoroughbreds. The other workers at the shop were teasing Ben about his dogs also. "They do what I want them to do," Ben said.

Ben caught a few coons at the first of the hunting season. There were a lot of leaves on the trees. The coons were hard to find in the trees. When all of the leaves had fallen off the trees, the coons began to run longer on the ground, and it became harder for the dogs to track them. Although it was hard for the dogs to track the coons, Ben was still having lots of luck catching coons. The guys with the expensive dogs were not catching any.

Some of the men at the plant wanted to know why Ben was catching coons with his dogs, and they weren't catching any; and they had good hunting dogs. The fellows would say that the reason they weren't able to catch the coons was because they went too far into the lake. Ben did not hunt around big lakes.

Ben would hunt by himself. Whenever he caught two coons in a night, he would quit hunting. Sometimes he had a hard time stopping his dogs from hunting. He would just go to his car and wait for them.

Hunting season was almost over. Ben's brother, Sam, had a friend that liked to hunt. His name was Tommy. Sam said to Tommy, "I have a brother that you would really like because he likes to hunt and fish and so do you. He doesn't drink and neither do you. I am going to give you his phone number. You will like him. You take this number and give him a call." Tommy took the number. He called Ben and said, "Ben, your brother Sam asked me to call you and ask you if you would let me go hunting with you."

Ben said, "You are welcome to go with me. I have a couple of dogs. They are not the best, but they will definitely tree a coon." Tommy said, "I don't have a dog." Ben said, "That's OK. You don't need licenses. We only carry one gun when we are hunting coons.

I have everything we need. What shift do you work?" Tommy replied, "The second shift." Ben said, "That's good. I work the same shift."

As the weeks passed by, the weather began to be permissible for hunting. Ben was glad that he had found someone to hunt with. Ben got off work earlier than Tommy, so he asked Tommy to call him when he got home. Tommy called Ben around 1:00 a.m.

After Ben received his call, he put his bag and gun in his van; then he took his flashlight and went to the dog pen to get his dogs. He let them roam around the backyard for about ten minutes; then he put them in the van.

Ben then got into the van himself and went to pick up Tommy. Then they headed for the woods. As they rode along, Tommy asked Ben if he thought they would catch a coon that night. "We will catch some if there are some out there to be caught," Ben said with a smile. Tommy replied, "I don't care if we catch a coon or not. As long as I can hear those dogs running, I'm happy."

Ben told him that he would take him where he could hear them run. "Are we going to a large cornfield?" Tommy asked. "There won't be any cornfields," Ben said. "But there will be some coons there. I will tell you the truth, I don't hunt in cornfields." Tommy said that, that's where the coons are because they go to the cornfields to get their food.

Ben said that in cornfields, you have to do too much walking. He told Tommy that he didn't care for a lot of walking; that was the reason he was going to take him to a place where the dogs will be running coons before they have a chance to walk 200 feet in the woods.

Tommy looked at him and laughed, then he said, "This I have got to see. All of the guys I ever hunted with, we did a lot of walking."

At this time, Ben had arrived at the woods where he hunted. He parked his van. He got out of the van and went to the back to let the dogs out. The dogs jumped out of the van and began to run around. Ben then got back in the van. He started putting on his hunting boots. Tommy asked, "Aren't you afraid that they will run off?" Ben said, "No, as a matter of fact, you will hear them running a coon in a few minutes." Tommy asked, "How will you know that they are running coons?" Ben said, "Don't worry, they aren't going to run anything else." While they were still talking, the dogs struck. They began to bark often. Tommy said, "We should be going before they get out of hearing range." Ben replied, "Don't worry, that coon is not going to run too far, as long as that old dog is behind him."

Tommy looked at Ben. He didn't say anything. He got out of the van and stood in front of it. Ben was still putting on his hunting jacket. Every so often Ben would holler to the dogs. The dogs were really barking up a storm. He knew that the dogs had found a coon. Tommy was on pins and needles because he knew that they were running something.

What Tommy didn't know was that Ben was an old pro at hunting. He had been hunting for a long time. He knew just the right moment to go after the dogs. He knew that the coons were just running in circles, but he was also watching the anticipation of Tommy. He knew that Tommy was anxious to get down to business. After the young dog treed, Ben said to Tommy, "Now we will go to them."

When they reached the dogs, only one was there at the tree. This tree was tall; the wind had blown it over. It had lodged in some smaller trees. The coon went up that tree and came down one of the other trees.

Ben looked at the tree; then he said, "This is an old coon. He isn't even in this tree." He walked over to the other trees where the top was large. He called the young dog. The dog came running over to him. Ben told the dog to find the coon. The dog started smelling around on the ground. Soon he picked up the track. Down through the woods he went just barking. Soon he treed again. They went over to the tree where Ring was barking. This tree was leaning over a lake. The tree had no leaves on it. The old dog was standing at the edge of the lake, looking out in the lake.

Ben stood there for a while watching the old dog who name was Blue. Tommy walked away from the tree, about two hundred feet away. Ben smiled to himself. Then he said to Ring, "Ring, the coon is not there, boy. He has jumped out of the tree and into the lake. Let's go somewhere else. This coon is too much for you."

Then he called to Tommy, "Let's go, this coon is too much for my dog." As they walked to the van, Tommy didn't say very much, but Ben had an idea of what might have been going through his mind. They soon reached the van; they loaded the dogs, then they got in. As Ben drove off, he said, "I hate to take a man out with me for the first time, and we don't catch a coon." He drove about another mile and half; then he pulled into a park on the side of the road.

Ben said, "What time do you have to be at home?" Tommy said that he didn't have to be home till 8:00 a.m. Tommy was telling Ben that he was going to take him to a place where they could catch some coons and that they wouldn't have to do a lot of walking. They got out of the van and walked across the road to a field. There they walked to a wooded area.

It was about four in the morning, and they were in the woods about fifteen minutes before the dogs were running again. Tommy went along with Ben, but he was dragging his feet. Ben knew that Tommy was disappointed in his dogs. The dogs that Tommy was used to hunting with did a lot of barking and caught few coons.

At this time, Blue and Ring were tracking slowly. Ben said, "Their track is cold. Give them a little time, and they will work it out." They stood still for twenty minutes and listened to the dogs running,

They began to bark more often now. Ben said that tracks have gotten hot. "Let's walk closer to the dogs," he said to Tommy. As they headed for the dogs, they were going straight away from them. Now their tracks must be tracking faster. They stopped for a few minutes to hear the dogs. The dogs had made a circle now; they were over to the left. So they turned and went left, and soon they had caught up with the dogs. They stopped a few yards back so as not to get too close. They could hear the dogs in the water hole to the left. They could also hear the coon running across in front of them, going to the water hole on their right. Tommy said, "What is that running on the ground in front of the dogs?" Ben said, "That's a family of coons running together." Tommy said, "What you mean, when you said that there was a family of coons running together?"

Ben said, "That's the mother and father and their young ones. They have three or four coons each time they breed."

The coons and dogs ran back and forth three times. The third time they went to the water hole on the right. The father coon had the mother coon and her young ones to go up a tree about half the distance between the water holes. The father coon would lead the dogs away from the tree. He went to the water hole on the right. There was a large tree lying across the water hole. He climbed up on that tree; the dogs could not jump up on this tree. After they had circled the water hole and could not pick up the coon's trail, the old came back to where the coon climbed up on the fallen tree and began to bark.

Ben said to Tommy, "Something is wrong because Blue is barking in one spot. Let us go to him."

Tommy said, "He has treed a coon." Ben told him, "No, he won't bark at a tree anymore. A couple of dogs whipped him at a tree once. I haven't been able to get him to tree since that night."

When they reached the water hole, Ben said that the father coon had tricked them again. He went to another tree. "See he went to this tree," Ben said, pointing to a tree close by. See all of those trees close and touching? That coon is up one of those trees."

Tommy said, "How are we going to find him?" Ben said, "We won't find him. One reason is that he is an old coon. He's not going to look at our light. There's another reason, and that is that he might be in his den. Don't you worry, Tommy. We will get a coon before we leave here." Tommy was in doubt; he didn't think they'd catch a coon that night.

Ben said, "Don't you worry. Give the dogs a little more time. They will find the tree those coons have gone to. They've gone up a tree somewhere around here." Tommy was thinking to himself, "Those dogs are no good. They do not bark like coonhounds." Then he said, "How are we going to find a coon when your old dog has quit treeing? And he is the one you are training the young dog with."

Ben said, "That old dog is going to track that coon to the tree, then he is going to rear up on it, then he will leave it."

Tommy did not say a word. The dogs left that water hole where Ben and Tommy were. Ben knew that those coons had gone up a tree somewhere close around.

Tommy walked about three hundred feet in the woods from Ben, heading toward the car. Ben kept checking those trees with his flashlight, trying to find a coon eye and watching Tommy at the same time. The young dog was barking about half the distance in between the two water holes. Ben did not hurry to go to him; he knew that he had treed the coons. He would call to the dog every so often to let him know that he had heard him. He walked closer to the dog, but stopped about one hundred feet from them. All the leaves were off the trees. It was a very small tree where the dogs were barking. Ben stood still and watched the dogs for about twenty minutes. He could also see the coons in the tree. The moon was shining in just a way where he could get a good view. He was also watching Tommy out of the corner of his eye. Tommy had found a tree and was leaning his back against the trees, looking nowhere in particular, just staring off into space.

Ben had come to the conclusion that Tommy didn't know much about hunting. Ben called Tommy with a loud voice, saying, "The coons are over here in the tree." That was sweet music to Tommy's ears. Tommy said, "How many is it?" Ben told him that it was two. Tommy then asked him, "Where were the dogs?" Ben told him that they were at the tree and asked him where did he think he'd be.

Tommy came through the woods as fast as he could walk at night with his light looking for the dogs. He did not stop walking until he had reached the dogs, shining his light on them.

Then he said with quite a bit of excitement, "He's got two feet on the tree!"

Ben stood back and watched Tommy. He could sense the excitement that Tommy was feeling. Then Tommy backed away from the tree so that he could get a better look up the tree. He shone his light up in the tree. He could see the coons. He then moved to another side of the tree where he could get still a better view of the coons.

Tommy said with a loud excited voice, "Can't you see, boy! It's three coons up this tree!" Ben then got excited and said, "Is it three? I only saw two." He walked closer to the tree so he could see. Tommy said, "Look at the meat up there," then he laughed. Ben said, "After I tie the old dog, we will shoot the coon out of the tree."

Tommy said, "We need him to help kill the coons when we shake them out of the tree." Ben said, "Don't you worry. Whenever that coon hits the ground, Ring will kill him, if you don't kill him when you shake him out of the tree. If both of them had been loose, they would tear those coons to pieces before we can get the coons from them good."

Tommy said, "This, I've got to see."

Ben tied old Blue about twenty feet from the tree. Then he walked around the tree looking up at the coons trying to find a good spot to stand to shoot the coons out of the tree.

Tommy said, "I can shoot them good from right here."

Ben said, "It will be better for you to shoot from this spot here," pointing at a spot directly across from where Tommy was already standing. "You can't shoot them from that position because the position that they're in, you won't be able to shoot them in the head. I want you to shoot them in the front legs. If you hit one of his front legs, he will not be able to crawl around in the tree without falling out."

Tommy came over where Ben was standing. Ben held the flashlight over Tommy's right shoulder, where he could see the coon better. Tommy aimed the gun at the part of the coon's body that Ben had told him to. Tommy pulled the trigger, and the gun fired, and down came one of the coons. As soon as the coon hit the ground, Ring ran over and caught him. Picked him up and ran around Ben and Tommy, taking the coon to his father, Blue. Blue grabbed hold of the coon. The poor coon's body never touched the ground. The coon was hollering; those dogs were tearing the coon's body apart. Ben tried to stop them, and Tommy just stood there looking in amazement. Ben made the young dog turn the coon loose, but he had to almost choke Blue loose from the coon. Then he put the coon in the bag.

Tommy said, "Man, those dogs are something. I have never seen dogs do what these dogs do. That old dog caught him a death hold on that coon and wouldn't let him go! Ben, this time we will stand over here near the old dog and shoot another coon out. I will keep the dogs from getting together. I will stay with the old dog. Come over here with me. You can hit one of the coons real good from over here." Tommy went over and stood and found him a good spot where he could shoot the coon. He raised his gun and aimed at the coon. Ben held the light. Tommy leaned, left shoulder against a tree to steady his body; then he took a shot at the tree. Down came the coon. Again, Ring grabbed the coon and headed for his father. Ben was standing by; he would not let them reach one another. Tommy just stood there laughing and watching the dogs. Ring was carrying a wounded coon around like he was a rag doll.

After Ring found out that Ben was not going to let Blue help him kill the coon, he stopped carrying him around and killed him. Tommy said, "Did you see that dog? He doesn't need any help killing coons." Ben said, "I know that he just love for his daddy to help him."

The coon was in the game bag. Now it was time for Tommy to shoot the third coon out of the tree. With all of the commotion that was going on, the third coon had made his way farther up the tree, and now it would be hard for Tommy to shoot him in the shoulder.

Ben said to Tommy, "Shoot this one anywhere you can. He will turn around. Then you can shoot him in the head." Tommy aimed and fired the gun. The bullet caught the tree in the right side. The coon couldn't go any higher, so he turned and started down the tree. Tommy was getting very anxious to shoot the coon out of the tree.

Ben said to Tommy, "Don't shoot the coon now. Wait until he passed by that fork in the tree." "Why not, I can hit him right in the head where he is now," said Tommy. Ben said, "If you wound him, he will get in the fork of the tree and die." "Oh no, he won't," Tommy said, aiming the gun at the tree. "I'm going to shoot this coon right out of his tree."

Ben said, "OK, that coon is yours. Now when you shoot him, and he climbs into the fork of that tree and die, you are going to climb up the tree and get him." Tommy said, "There's no need for all of that because I'm going to shoot him right out of the tree."

"We will see," said Ben. Tommy shot the gun. The coon fell about two feet, caught himself, and crawled into the fork of the tree. Ben said, "That is as far as he's going to go. Now he will die in that fork of the tree." Tommy said, "I will keep shooting him until he falls out."

Ben let Tommy shoot the coon about ten times. Ben said, "That coon is dead. Don't you see that when you shoot him he does not move? The only way that you will get him out of that fork, is to climb up and get him." Tommy began climbing the tree. He got about six feet from the coon; then he said, "This is as far as I go." Ben said, "Stay there, I will get you a stick to push him out of the tree." Ben passed a stick to Tommy, one that he could handle with one hand. Tommy took the stick, holding to the tree with one hand and pushing the coon with the stick. It took him about fifteen minutes to push that coon out of the fork of that tree. After he pushed the coon out of the tree, he jumped down himself.

Ben told him that the more they catch coons, the more he'll learn about coons. Tommy replied, "I have learned a lot tonight." Ben said, "Now we can go home. I hate to take someone hunting, and we do not catch a coon on the first time." Tommy spoke, "Man, those are some good dogs you have. There's not but one thing wrong, and that is you just don't hunt them enough."

They put all the coons in the game bag and headed for home. Ben was saying that they should have gotten four coons. He said that there was another coon somewhere around there. Tommy told him that he should be happy with the ones they did catch.

Ben said, "I am, but I do want that fourth coon." Tommy replied, "Man, I am well pleased. I have seen more coons with these dogs in one night than those other guys I was hunting with the whole hunting season." Ben had his dogs under pretty good control. He called them and said, "Let's go home, boys." As they headed for the car, Ben said to Tommy, "Keep an eye on Blue, and we will get that fourth coon." He came down this way. It was daylight now; they could see the dogs, a good ways off. Old Blue started through the woods ahead of them, his head close to the ground. He started going back and forth; then he went through the woods real fast.

Ben watched him. "He has picked up that fourth coon's tracks," said Ben. "If we can keep close on him, we will see him when he goes to the tree." Blue went about 300 feet then he reared up on a tree. He jumped down and made a complete circle around the tree, then he came back. Again he reared up on the tree. There was a coon sitting on the first limb of the tree with his tail hanging down. Tommy just stood there and watched Blue. Blue took his feet off the tree, turned, and walked away.

Tommy hollered, "Did you see that? That dog was looking at that coon, and he wouldn't even bark. Now that dog is just plain dirty." Ben said, "He used to be the best tree dog that I had. Now I can't make him bark at a tree." Tommy said, "I will shoot this one out then we will go home. This bag is getting heavy."

On their way home, Tommy was one happy man. Tommy said, "I like hunting with these dogs. You don't have to walk far. Just wait until I go to work, I got something to tell the boys."

Before Ben and Tommy got another chance to go hunting, the snow fell. That was the last hunting that Blue and Ring did. Ben took Ring to the vet to get him dewormed. The doctor gave him a shot, and it killed him. The same day, Blue was tied beside a six-foot fence. He climbed over the fence and hung himself. Now they have no coon dogs. The next fall, Ben was able to buy one of Ring's sisters back. This little dog made history.

Blue's and Ring's last hunt

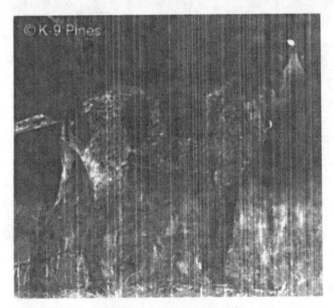

Bluetick Coonhound

An Angry Raccoon

AN ANGRY RACCOON

An angry coon met face-to-face
With a game-hungry man
Boy, oh boy, what a fight it was.
They fought and fought.
There was a knockdown in the first round.
The fight was a long way from being over.
The second knockdown, one fighter
Was saved by dog and not by
The bell.

In the year of 1977, Ted was no longer hunting rabbits. Rabbits were scarce in the state of Michigan. Raccoons were plentiful. Ted started hunting coons. He had a bluetick hound that weighed seventy pounds. Her name was Fannie. He often said that she was worth her weight in gold.

In the month of September, on the second Saturday, Ted, Bob, and Sam took their dogs out that morning at nine o'clock to chase coons. The sun was shining bright, and there were no clouds in the sky. The men were taking their dogs out, so Fannie could train them to hunt coons. Training season had begun. They wanted their dogs to know how to hunt.

Bob's hound was a black-and-tan female, and Sam's hound was a pretty male bluetick; the dogs were grown.

They knew that Fannie could train them. She was one of the best hunting dogs in the state of Michigan. They knew that.

Ted picked them up that morning. As they traveled along the highway, Bob asked where would they find a coon in the daytime. They only traveled at night.

Ted laughed, "Haw haw haw." Then he said, "We will find some coons walking around today."

"This, I want to see," Bob replied.

Sam turned sideways in his seat and said, "I have hunted coons most of my life. This is the first time I have ever heard of *hunting* coons in the daytime. I am going just for the ride!"

Ted replied, "You see that little dog in the back of the truck? She will start tracking a coon within twenty minutes after we enter the woods."

Big Bob leaned back in his seat, stretched, and said, "I don't care where we go. I believe what the man said. He never told me a lie about coon hunting. Don't ever play him and that little dog cheap, they will make an ass out of you every time."

Ted laughed, "Haw haw haw." Then he answered Sam's question, "We are going to Bald Mountain."

Sam started laughing, and he laughed. Every time he looked at Ted, he would laugh harder and harder. When he reached the point that he could not stop laughing. He said, "There are no coons out there." Then, he called Bob and asked, "Do you remember how we hunted out there? Our dogs never found a coon track, nor a coon. Now I know we are wasting our time."

Bob raised his voice roaring like a lion, saying, "Man, I told you to keep your mouth shut, loudmouth!"

Ted was driving and listening and smiling to himself knowing that Sam's mouth would soon be closed. Soon, he reached his hunting spot and parked the truck. He said, "We will hunt here."

Sam yelled, "Man, you parked in the wrong place. The large woods is on the other side of the road."

Ted recited, "The coons are over here. You can go to the woods or follow Fannie and me."

Sam uttered, "This, I got to see."

Big Bob screamed, "Man, you better shut up and listen to the man."

Ted opened the back door of the van and let the dogs out. Then, he headed toward those scattered trees on the side of a hill. At the bottom of it, there was a stream of water, eight feet wide, sixteen inches deep. This water was clear as crystal. The pretty green grass was turning brown. The pretty oak tree leaves were turning brown. Before they could reach the water, they could hear Fannie barking.

Sam hollered, "She has jumped a rabbit, Ted."

"She's not running rabbits," Ted replied. "Do you hear her running in and out of the water? Rabbits do not run in water like that. That's a coon. I will stake my life on it."

Sam laughed, "Haw haw haw." Then he grunted, "Um um um." Then, he said, "You don't care about your life. I would not bet my life on no dog."

Ted turned and spoke these words, "Do you hear that dog running in and out of the water? That's a coon she's trailing. Just listen at her talking to me." Then, he hollered "Whooo," to let her know that he was listening.

Sam said, "She's running the hell out that rabbit."

She was running like a ball of fire, going down the stream of water.

"We will have to try to keep up with her, where the other dogs will start following her, if you all want them to learn how to track a coon," Ted replied.

They walked through the woods to the stream of water following the dog. The faster they walked, the farther away she got. They walked through the underbrush, out in an open field, where they could walk faster. The grass was four feet tall. The dog trailed the coon down to the stream to where another stream of water ran into it. This stream came from the trout pond. On the left hand side of the field, the water streams together in the shape of the alphabet letter Y, with this field of grass in the middle of it. The coon went up the other stream to the trout pond, with the dog following. They cut across the field to get closer to her. When they reached the other stream, they had reached the pond.

Ted said, "We can't walk fast enough to catch up. We will wait here for them to come back."

Soon they heard Fannie coming back. Ted knew that the coon was in front of her. He came out of the water about twenty feet above them into the grass. That little dog was on his trail, barking like a puppy. They made a large circle in the tall grass. Bob did his best to get his dog to help her. Sam looked at Pretty Boy and said, "He doesn't feel like hunting."

Ted replied, "Just listen. She doesn't need any help, that coon better run. If he doesn't, he is going to get caught." He got tired of running and turned to fight. Oh, what a noise they made. He made up his mind that he was not going to run anymore. This was his territory. He was the boss. He was not climbing a tree, nor was he running anymore. Soon the other dogs heard them fighting. They rushed in to help.

Sam cried out, "That coon, she got him. We got to help before he gets away."

Ted spoke softly, "Do not worry. He's not going anywhere." Every time he turned to run, that little dog would catch his rear end and pull him back. "All we have in our hands is a dog chain. I will cut me a stick."

All the dogs were barking; the coon was growling and hollering. Fannie with her lead voice, "Yo yoo yoooo." Sue was baritone, "How hoow hooow." Pretty Boy with a deep base, "Whoo, whooo, whoooo."

That was music to the ears of the hunters. Big Bob was doing a dance like you've never seen before, standing in one spot, his feet and arms moving, his stomach shaking like a bowl of jelly, and laughing. He was having a ball.

Ted was cutting himself a stick. Sam was watching and listening to their dogs, showing all thirty-two teeth, with a hungry look on his face. In his mind, that was bacon on his table. He could not let him get away. The noise was getting to him. He started jumping up and down. All at once, he cried out with a loud voice, "They are going to let him get away."

Ted turned to talk to him. He had moved like a flash of lightning. His body was bouncing like a ball. Soon he was standing beside the ring, looking at the coon. Each dog was taking turns biting the coon. They had wallowed the grass down, making a five feet by five. Every dog that came into the ring, he would run them out.

The coon moved to the center of the ring, looking up at Sam with a hump in his back. His eyes were saying, "Come in you big black bull. I will kick your ass too."

Sam stood there looking. All at once, he leaped on Mr. Coon's back, pinning his head to the ground. With his right foot, he reached down with his right hand, grabbing hold of his tail and lifting his rear end off the ground. He looked back over his left shoulder at Ted. In his mind, this was meat on his table. Then, he cried out with a loud voice, saying, "That's all right, Ted. I have him. My foot is on his head and his tail in my hand."

Ted could not believe his eyes or ears. This was the first time he had seen a man catch a live coon. He kept on cutting his stick, going through his mind. What is he going to do when the dog pulls him from underneath his foot? He knew that Fannie was going to do that. He looked up again. She had pulled the coon's head from underneath his foot. There he stood holding a live coon by the tail high in the air. Soon his front part was moving up his tail. Bad Sam let go. He fell to the ground; he stood up on his back legs and began to walk like a man heading straight for Sam. He turned to run and fell. He started crawling on his hands and knees, looking back over his shoulder. His head parted the grass like a cow. The coon got down on all four feet. Before he could leap on Sam's back, Fannie caught hold of him. He turned to fight. She let go and ran. Sam crawled about twenty feet away, sat down, and yelled, "You all can have him. I don't want him."

Ted knew that it was his turn now. Big Bob was not going close to that ring. The dogs were standing back in the grass baying at the coon. Mr. Raccoon was real angry. He was running all over the ring, making a loud noise, daring anyone to enter. Pretty Boy with his deep voice went "Whooo," sticking his head in the ring. The coon ran over and grabbed hold of the right side of his mouth. He stood there hollering. Fannie ran over, grabbing the coon's rear end, pulling both of them to the other side before the coon let go and chased after her. She ran back in the grass. He turned to see where Jerry was. He was walking out of the ring. That coon rushed over and grabbed him by his left hind leg. Jerry stood with his leg sticking back hollering. Ted walked slowly as he headed to the ring, passing by Bob and Sam. Soon he was looking down on Mr. Coon. The dogs stood in the grass watching him.

The coon looked up at Ted and moved over to the other side, putting a hump in his back, making loud noises, saying, "I have to whip your dogs. Kicked that black bull so until he couldn't stand up. I am the king of this jungle. Don't make me wait."

Ted knew that he had to do something, and he had to do it fast. The coon could have run away. He took his stick off his shoulder, bringing it down on the coon again and again. He kept doing this until the coon was flat on the ground. He picked up the coon, carried him over to Sam, laid it down, saying, "Here is your coon."

Sam laughed, "Haw haw haw." Then, he said, "This was some coon. Man, oh man, I thought I was a goner. Fannie saved my life."

Ted looked over at Bob, who was sitting on the ground. He had danced until his legs gave out.

CPSIA information can be obtained at www.ICGtesting.com
Printed in the USA
LVOW081847100413

328571LV00001B/199/P